JUDGES AND POLITICS IN THE CONTEMPORARY AGE

JUDGES AND POLITICS IN THE CONTEMPORARY AGE

RICHARD HODDER-WILLIAMS

Bowerdean Briefings
SERIES EDITOR: PETER COLLINS

BOWERDEAN
Publishing Company Limited

First published in 1996 by the Bowerdean Publishing Company Ltd.
of 8 Abbotstone Road, London SW15 1QR

British Library Cataloguing-in-Publication Data.
A catalogue record for this book is available from the British Library.

ISBN 0 906097 39 8

Designed by the Senate.

Printed in Malta by Interprint Limited

CONTENTS

For Rhiain, who has had to wait too long for a dedication and who has had to put up with judges and politics at antisocial moments.

PREFACE

Over the last twenty years in Britain, the senior judges have found themselves reported upon and evaluated in the nation's press to a degree that is both new and requiring of comment. I am not thinking simply of Sir Richard Scott's enquiry (although that is important) but rather the actions of ministers and other public officials that have been challenged in the courts and, on occasions, have been dramatically quashed. While Michael Howard, the Home Secretary in 1996, may have felt especially belaboured, he has by no means been alone. People have been more able, and more willing, to seek a judicial review of administrative action to which they have taken exception and their complaints have found their ways through the courts to the media. By finding the behaviour of ministers (or elected local officials) illegal, judges had clearly entered the political scene. Naturally, and rightly, the propriety of this became a matter of debate and disagreement. The *Sunday Times* made one judgement with the striking headline: 'Too big for their wigs'.

Elsewhere in Europe, courts have also been active in the political fray, in the sense that they have struck down laws and regulations passed by duly elected politicians. The readiness of the European Courts in Strasbourg and Luxembourg to find the actions of British public servants illegal is obvious to the reader of the broadsheets. But the readiness of the German Constitutional Court or the French *Conseil Constitutionel* to do the same receives rather less attention. There appears to have been a growing readiness, and not only in the United Kingdom, for judges to exercise their judicial power in ways that have a direct and important effect on the governance of countries. Some have called this the 'judicialisation of politics', suggesting a definite tendency for an increasing number of decisions formerly taken exclusively within the overtly political branches of government to be taken, instead, by unelected judges answerable to no electorate.

It is interesting to speculate on why this might be. It is surely connected with the relative failure of the political process to meet the aspirations of those who are governed under it and with the rise of the administrative state and a bevy of bureaucracies the decisions of which affect so much of so many people's lives. It is surely also connected with a more educated, more challenging electorate that is less deferential to government in all its forms and is more aware of deficiencies through a lively, and often vulgar, press. In addition, it is surely connected with an ideological shift throughout Europe, which has enhanced the status of rights-based demands and has redefined a substantial part of what politics is about, away from struggles between classes and religious groups towards conflict between the coercive powers of the state and the individual. And it must be connected, finally, with particular individuals within the judiciaries, men like Lord Denning in Britain or Earl Warren in the United States, who had the strength of character and self-belief to challenge the old orthodoxies and help usher in new values and expectations.

Be that as it may, the rise to prominence of judges may seem new to Europeans (among whom I count the British), but it is, of course, not new to the citizens of the United States of America. 150 years ago that perceptive French aristocrat Alexis de Tocqueville had observed that there was scarcely a question that divided the American people which did not end up in the

Supreme Court for resolution. In the last half century, that Court has pronounced authoritatively on the segregatory practices of the southern states, on the rights of suspects, on the separation of church and state, on the limits of gender equality, on a woman's right to an abortion, on the reach of a president's claim to executive privilege, and on a host of matters affecting civil rights, social security, bankruptcy laws, and more. Anybody interested in the interplay between the judicial and political functions of a contemporary democracy must look a good deal at the United States. And that is exactly what I shall be doing.

However, we should not be carried away by the very real changes that are taking place in the United Kingdom in relations between courts and politicians to imagine that there is under way an inexorable movement towards an 'imperial judiciary' (as Nathan Glazer once described the US Supreme Court). The vast majority of political decisions on both sides of the Atlantic are still taken by elected politicians and their advisers within the great departments of state. The critical economic choices reflecting tax levels and expenditure patterns, the foreign policy decisions involving a nation's security and contribution to world politics, and the major contours of social policies remain unquestionably within the domain of the legislative and executive branches of government. There is no need to get overly alarmed that judges have made a pitch to run the public affairs of the nation.

Nevertheless, the shifting balance between the judicial and the political institutions of government is important. It is important, I think, not only because it reflects important changes – both empirical and normative – in our political systems but also because a great deal of what is written and said seems to me to be misguided and frequently simplistic. This book is intended to set the debate in a context that is readily comprehensible to any interested and intelligent citizen. It is not primarily intended for my academic colleagues. To those whose study of the law and judicial procedures is an all absorbing and full-time concern, I make an unapologetic apology; I know that there are places where I have glossed over some complexities, that there are cases that do not fit neatly into some of my analyses, and that there is still a great deal more that could be said. But I hope that the following chapters put into a useful perspective the very important, and contested, arguments that currently rage about the relationships between judges and politics. I hope, too, that it will kindle in some readers a new fascination with the profound, and difficult, questions involved in deciding how best to run a liberal democracy in the twenty-first century.

Richard Hodder-Williams
Bristol, March 1996

I

JUDGES AS NECESSITIES

Late in 1995 the British newspapers were full of stories about conflict between the Conservative government, especially its Home Secretary Michael Howard, and the nation's judges. There were three separate dimensions to these stories. The most strident reports drew attention to the increasing regularity with which the courts found the actions of ministers illegal. Between November 1994 and November 1995 judges quashed Mr Howard's decision that two Kashmiri students should serve a minimum of 25 years for the murder of an Indian diplomat rather than the initial ten (subsequently increased to 20 by the previous Home Secretary, Kenneth Clarke), ordered Mr Howard to disclose against his wishes expert advice he had received before deciding whether to refer alleged miscarriages of justice to the appeal court, hastened Mr Howard's decision to refer some cases to the appeal court under the clear threat that legal proceedings would have compelled him to do so, reversed (to Mr Howard's chagrin) a ban on temporary leave for prisoners to consult their lawyers, ruled, by three votes to two, that Mr Howard's introduction of a tariff–based criminal injuries compensation scheme without reference to Parliament was an abuse of the prerogative power, ruled that Mr Howard's six-month delay in considering a parole application by five IRA prisoners was unreasonable and unlawful and overthrew Mr Howard's decision to ban Sun Myung Moon from Britain without a hearing. While Mr Howard and his Home Office took the brunt of the judges' activism, he was not alone. The Foreign Secretary, Douglas Hurd, had been smartly rapped over the knuckles for ignoring the principles set down in statute for the Overseas Development Administration's aid programmes providing financial support for the Pergau dam in Malaysia, in return, so it was said, for a substantial order for military equipment.

A second, more circumspect, set of stories observed that senior judges were no longer content to operate discretely out of the public gaze. Now, they were open in their criticism of what the government was planning to do. The highest court in the United Kingdom is the Judicial Committee of the House of Lords, which is precisely what it says it is, a committee whose members sit in the House of Lords. The Committee, composed formally of eleven Lords of Appeal in Ordinary, usually sits in panels of five and the conclusions of its deliberations are marked not with a formal opinion (or opinions) but with speeches. That, at any rate, is the fiction. In fact, although its members technically do not hand down opinions but publish speeches, the effect is the same, even if the language is different, because these 'speeches' are not actually spoken but printed! In these written explanations of their decisions, the Law Lords will inevitably criticize government action, if only implicitly, whenever they decide against it, but they do it out of the public eye and in measured, legal prose. This, it is widely felt, is the proper, and probably the complete, role for the Committee.

However, the Law Lords have increasingly been using their positions as members of the House of Lords to participate actively in the legislative process by contributing trenchant speeches, especially, but not exclusively, on bills that affect the judicial system. They have, for example, been at the forefront of the movement to incorporate the European Convention of

Human Rights into British law. They are well aware that the government record before the European Court of Human Rights in Strasbourg has not been good. Between 1966 and 1995 Britain suffered 31 reversals out of 45 cases, a record matched by no other signatory. In 1996 Britain and Ireland were the only two countries out of the 38 Council of Europe members not to have incorporated the Convention into domestic law or inaugurated a national Bill of Rights. In the view of several senior judges, both retired and active, those Strasbourg rulings embarrass the governing and legal classes; they postpone justice for an unacceptably long time and they are absurdly expensive. It would be much better, they argue, if British judges applied the Convention in line with the European Court's precedents rather than continue to deal with issues of human rights under British precedents and in a system lacking a codified Bill of Rights, knowing that they are likely to be overruled once the laborious progress through the European courts is complete.

The senior judges have also lobbied ministers, especially on matters concerned with sentencing, where their desire for the continuation of a judge's discretion and flexibility (within the parameters circumscribed by statute, of course) runs counter to the Minister's commitment to fixed and heavy penalties. When Mr Howard made public his intention to establish mandatory penalties for some multiple offenders, senior judges responded instantly and publicly, especially some of those who had only recently retired from office. Their criticism could be largely ignored because, however eminent and experienced they might have been, they could be made to appear of no greater importance than any other citizens. More significant was the intervention of the then Lord Chief Justice, Lord Taylor of Gosforth, who immediately criticized the proposed reduction in judges' discretion on sentencing, and the Judges' Council, a committee composed of the heads of the High Court's divisions, placed the item on its agenda. To many conservative critics, such behaviour compromised a central constitutional principle of the separation of powers and trespassed on the preserve of politicians in a manner that was inappropriate and, in the last analysis, undemocratic. To those critics, the judges seemed, as a *Sunday Times* headline had it, to have become 'too big for their wigs'.

Disagreements between judges and politicians were not kept to the genteel confines of a single pointed sentence in a speech or an off-the-record comment to an interested journalist. They were catapulted into the open through a carefully instigated debate in the House of Lords and subsequent comment in the media. The Lord Chief Justice, a few weeks before a retirement forced upon him by ill health, made a substantial and obviously deeply felt contribution which went beyond matters of judicial organization (for which he has considerable responsibilities) to matters of public policy. He argued, as any member of one house of Parliament is constitutionally entitled to do, that the government's penal policy was founded on a misreading of the evidence, would be counterproductive and impinged upon the judicial role. The politician's responses combined natural defences of the policy itself with attacks on the Chief Justice for straying beyond his proper judicial role. The debate thus raised very directly important constitutional issues about the relationship between judges and politicians.

A third set of stories were more philosophical and more concerned with general questions of the judges' proper position in the country's constitutional order. Leader writers could not but be aware of the politicians' dismay, indeed anger, at the judges' behaviour. This was a view that was not the exclusive preserve of the Conservative Party; leading figures in the Labour

Party were also ready to challenge the judges and urge them to be more self-restrained. Lord Irvine, the shadow Lord Chancellor, quite explicitly warned the judges to be so. He may have had good reason to take this line. When the Party had last held office, between 1974 and 1979, the Judicial Committee of the House of Lords had struck down several regulations passed by Labour authorities. It was also a position that somebody hopeful of acquiring power and the full panoply of authority provided by the sovereignty of parliament would likely take. Perhaps that is too cynical a view.

The publicized conflict in Britain between bench and politician was not entirely new, although it did seem to have reached a new pitch of passion and regularity. We must accept that it is highly likely, if not inevitable, in any system of government presuming to be guided by the 'rule of law' that the judiciary will, from time to time, come into conflict with the government of the day. Observers of the judicial scene had noted a decade or more earlier how the courts had handed down decisions that appeared highly political and often contrary to the wishes of the elected government. Most of this new activism stemmed from a greater readiness of citizens, lawyers and public interest groups to seek what is formally referred to as 'a judicial review of administration'. In layman's language, these litigants argue that a minister or some official acting on behalf of the state behaved in a manner that was beyond his or her powers or against the notion of natural justice.

Alongside the greater readiness to seek judicial review has been a greater preparedness of the judges to accede to such requests. In part, the increased visibility of the judicial role can be explained by societal change and a shift in judicial philosophy that persuaded individual judges to ease access. But there is a much more principled reason and one that is, in reality, deeply embedded in the British common law tradition and the British commitment to 'the rule of law'.

If individuals are governed ultimately by laws rather than the momentary fancies of the powerful, they need a place to challenge the exercise of those laws when ministers or their subordinates appear to have exceeded their authority as laid down specifically in statutes. If individuals are thought to enjoy some civil and political rights, they need a place to assert and protect them. Courts are those places. And the judges must adjudicate between the government and its challengers. Sometimes – often, in the eyes of their critics – governments do overstep their legal powers or deny individuals their rights. If the critics are correct, courts are obliged to restrain the politicians, a restraint to which ministers do not naturally take kindly.

It was not only judges in Britain who felt the wrath of the popular press and the criticisms of vocal back benchers. The judges of the European Court of Human Rights regularly found the British Government in breach of its obligations under the European Convention on Human Rights, which was established way back in 1953 with the United Kingdom as one of its initial signatories, and many a Eurosceptic, thinking erroneously that this was all further evidence of the European Union's institutions attacking British sovereignty, demanded that Britain pull out of the Convention altogether. Naturally, when the European Court in Luxembourg, which is responsible for adjudicating on the legality of governmental actions in the light of the Treaty of Rome, found against the United Kingdom, the Eurosceptics had another field day. At least, on this occasion the focus of their ire was indeed an institution of the European Union. Other governments had also had laws affecting their own citizens held unlawful, but this made few, if any, ripples on the media.

The criticism brought into the open a central, and not easily resolved, problem of all systems that claim to be governed by law. The Treaty of Rome and its progeny, such as the Maastricht Treaty, binds its signatories to a set of rules, some of which are not always clear enough to cover every eventuality. Where there is a dispute, either because a government has failed to honour its obligations under the Treaties or because there is a genuine disagreement on the legality of a Commission decision, two options are open to the member states. In one, strength prevails and governments do what they wish if they can get away with it; in the other, law prevails and courts make the adjudication, which is binding on all the parties. It really is very difficult to make an association of states work even tolerably well if some of its members feel able to decide unilaterally on the rights and wrongs of their, and other states', actions as it pleases them. All associations involve, in return for gains unattainable without the association, a necessary derogation from absolute freedom or sovereignty; it is as true of marriage as of international organizations. And both fall apart if this is not recognized.

The public awareness of the importance of courts, whether in Europe or in London, was a special feature of the British scene in 1995 and 1996 particularly, but the lack of congruity between the actions of courts and the desires of vocal and active citizens was by no means confined to Britain. Simultaneously with the British furore, Germans, too, were becoming incensed with some of their judiciary. A Bavarian court had upheld the claim that states within the German Republic could not require a crucifix to be placed in every classroom in their schools, because it transgressed the freedom of religion clause of the country's Basic Law. Twenty thousand angry Bavarians, Protestant as well as

Catholic, protested in Munich against the judgement, which appeared to nullify the preferences of the people as expressed through the majoritarian structures of democratic politics. A few years earlier in France, the *Conseil Constitutionel* had dramatically increased its political significance by arrogating to itself a role that was manifestly not explicit in the Constitution. In 1971, it struck down a bill that radically limited freedom of political association, arguing that the Preamble to the 1958 Constitution incorporated all the rights set out in the 1789 Declaration of the Rights of Man and additional rights set out in the preamble to the Fourth Republic's Constitution. Never before had these rights been considered judicially protected. This daring acquisition of power soon resulted in the *Conseil* being the place in which individuals claimed their rights, and by 1987 as much as 40 per cent of the laws nullified were done so on the grounds that they denied people their fundamental rights.

Whether the conflict between judges and politicians in the United Kingdom is new in quality or merely quantity, neither it nor the assertion of judicial power in countries such as France and Germany can compare with the centrality of the federal courts in the United States. Political passions have regularly been roused by judges seemingly second guessing the duly elected representatives of the American people and denying them the fruits of their electoral victories. In the 1930s, the Supreme Court hacked away at President Roosevelt's New Deal programme, designed to combat the appalling consequences of the Wall Street Crash and the ensuing Depression; in the 1950s, the Supreme Court found that segregation – the social cement and symbol of the white South – was no longer constitutional; in the 1970s, the Supreme Court discovered, in *Roe v. Wade,* a woman's fundamental right to an abortion and, momentarily at least, found capital punishment to be unconstitutional.

The political response was in all cases immediate and explicit. For a brief moment, Roosevelt toyed with recasting the Court by increasing its size from 9 to 15 Justices (thus permitting him to ensure a majority for his way of thinking). In the 1950s, the chief judges of the states signed a general criticism of what they saw as the Supreme Court's legislative ambitions and the southern states embarked upon a policy of massive disobedience; some politicians tried to impeach the chief justice himself. In the 1980s, Republicans tried in vain to amend the Constitution in order to reverse some of the Supreme Court's actions and critical politicians carefully orchestrated an attack on its jurisprudence. A person's position on abortion could affect chances of election or nomination to a federal judgeship and opponents of the Supreme Court's decision took to picketing abortion clinics, then to bombing them, and later even to shooting the doctors working in them.

I could go round a host of other countries to exemplify the tension between politicians and judges and to illustrate both the reality of judges striking down as unconstitutional or illegal the actions of elected politicians and the rising intensity of the political response. This book is designed to explain why this should not be a surprise to us and why much of the comment about the performance of judges is often misplaced and simplistic. At the same time, central questions for a democracy are starkly raised and demand an answer. The following pages are intended to address this issue, too, and to suggest that many interpretations of the democratic ideal can only be realized with a judiciary that uses its power to negate the aspirations of elected politicians.

The State and the Purpose of Laws

Before we get fully into the judgmental mode, we need to start at the beginning and seek an answer to that central question of political theory: what is the state for? The human race is a quarrelsome body of people. It also seems to be highly competitive, constantly seeking advantages over neighbours and rivals. This is the well spring of politics. If there were no disagreements – no quarrels, no competition – there would be no politics. For politics is a ubiquitous human activity the purpose of which is nothing less, and little more, than managing disagreements that are not amenable to simple objective resolution. Politics is mostly associated with the state, but you will find it in smaller organizations, in Women's Institutes and cricket clubs, and even in families. Indeed, wherever there is disagreement within a group that needs management, but for which there are no objective and agreed rules for its resolution, there will you find politics. Arguments over the length of a piece of string or the weight of a cake can be resolved quite simply with a measuring tape or a set of scales. But arguments over where we should go for a holiday, or who should be captain of the team, or how much tax we should pay, or what constitutes pornography, or what land we have a moral claim to, are not susceptible to such easy solutions; they have no relevant indices of measurement against which rival claims can be weighed. It is through politics that such questions must be resolved.

Much has been imagined and written about the causes and development of established political processes. Once upon a time, perhaps, sheer strength and physical power resolved disputes; power *was* right. At some stage in human development, it has been surmised, people came to the conclusion that this was not a satisfactory way of deciding many matters about which there were disagreements. The strongest, after all, may not always be the wisest and the costs of imposing solutions through physical force are usually high. Consequently, societies came to evolve rules that governed the way disputes were handled and that established accepted and expected modes of behaviour. These rules were initially understandings or conventions that members of society knew and learned and accepted as the proper way to deal with disagreements. Later, many of the rules were written down in laws and the most important ones into constitutions.

It is essential to be quite clear about what governments actually do when they pass laws or promulgate regulations on the basis of laws. There are two critical dimensions of their actions that need emphasizing again. The first is that all laws are effectively expressions of values, choices between alternatives, which are made, not on an objective basis testable by the highly skilled but on a subjective scale, reflecting the priorities and ideals of the government members and their followers. The second is that those who control the institutions of the state have the legal authority, and in the most successful political systems the moral authority, to impose these choices upon the inhabitants of that state. The values that find expression in laws have the authority of the state to back them and the state's powers − police, tax officials, civil servants − are empowered to enforce those choices, by coercion if necessary. We may say, then, that politics is the process by which an authoritative allocation of values is made for the people within a state.

Precisely how these choices were made has differed from state to state and from epoch to epoch. There have naturally been some systems that leant more heavily towards physical power and others that were largely ordered through rules. Clearly, too, some societies developed a highly sophisticated set of procedures for dispute resolution long before others did. We have only to compare the city states of Greece, especially Athens, with medieval England to see the difference. But even in the days of King John there were rules, not particularly egalitarian or humane, no doubt, but rules nonetheless, which people broke to their disadvantage. The King's emissaries and judges were designed to ensure that the King's word was upheld and that his understanding of the rules prevailed. Judges heard evidence between disputants, decided whether the law had, in fact, been broken, and sentenced the guilty party, if there was one, to due punishment. Judges, for the most part, are still envisaged as people who decide upon guilt and innocence and then ordain the punishment for the guilty. They still do so. It was precisely on the issue of sentencing powers that the senior judges in Britain quarrelled with Conservative politicians in 1995 and 1996.

The state is not only a geographic space. It is also, as I have suggested, a set of institutions that claims the authority to impose on the inhabitants within its jurisdiction, by coercion if necessary, the duty to obey the laws and regulations made in its name. It is through these institutions that those coercive powers are defined, legitimated, and exercised. In all but a few countries, and certainly in all countries that claim to be democracies, there are inevitably disagreements over the exact meaning of some constitutional provisions, or the precise reach of a power delegated to a state official, or the detailed rights of an individual in a particular situation. Often, these disagreements are wilful and derive from nothing more than a partisan opposition to the laws and regulations promulgated on behalf of the state by a set of politicians to whom the complainant is politically opposed. But sometimes the disagreement is more problematic, more idealistic, more general. The human capacity to provide with absolute clarity against every eventuality is sadly inadequate, so that there will always be disagreement over the meaning of words.

Take, for example, the section 1(1) of the Transport (London) Act, which laid upon the Greater London Council, in the days when such a body existed, the duty to provide 'integrated, efficient and economic transport facilities and services in Greater London'. What is meant here by economic? The Greater London Council maintained that it meant cost-effective, implying that transport facilities might have wider purposes than merely carrying commuters as cheaply as possible from home to work; it might have social purposes, such as providing opportunities for the poor and elderly to travel cheaply, or environmental purposes, such as encouraging more people on to the transport system in order to reduce car traffic and the accompanying pollution. So the Council reduced the fares, knowing the system as a whole would make a loss, and increased the level of property taxes (or rates) in order to make good the shortfall. For so long as the policies were indeed effective for their purposes, which were social and environmental in part, they were legal. The Bromley District Council objected. Its interpretation of the word economic was that any business to which the adjective was applied should, taking one year with another, break even financially. Hence, a transport system that was knowingly not self-financing and which demanded additional subsidies from ratepayers could not be economic as required by the Act. So the meaning given by the Greater London Council, controlled by the Labour Party, was pitted against the meaning given by the London Borough of Bromley, controlled by the Conservative Party. Whichever way the judges went, they were going to antagonize one major political party or the other. In the event, they angered the Labour politicians.

The rule of law abhors arbitrariness. Indeed, one purpose of law is to make clear and explicit what is demanded of the inhabitants of a state and what the officials acting in the state's name may (and conversely may not) do to ensure that the positive requirements of the law are met. The goal is clarity and certainty, but this is often not achieved. Sometimes, of course, this is due to poor drafting, but often it is due to a genuine disagreement over the precise meaning of certain words or over its application in the face of a set of facts that the law-makers had never envisaged. But the rule of law and the philosophy of liberalism that underpins contemporary *liberal* democracy also presumes that individuals have rights that politicians cannot abridge, rights without which the state would be neither liberal nor democratic.

Two observations are necessary at this stage. First, even in the liberal democracies with which we most closely identify and admire, those who win positions of authority within the state's structure do not always act with propriety and entirely within the limitations laid down by law. Many citizens, even in the most civilized and progressive countries, feel deeply that they have been improperly treated by agents of the state and they need a forum in which to seek redress. Second, rights are slippery things. Some countries consciously seek to protect a limited number of specified civil and political rights by enshrining them in a Bill of Rights, which is superior in status to the ordinary laws of the land passed by legislatures and is judicially enforced. Others do not escalate rights to such a preferred position nor do they always make them explicitly enforceable in courts of law. But there has been a very clear momentum over the last half-century towards both an enunciation of individual rights in documents of superior status to ordinary laws and a practice of granting to courts, either explicitly or by default, the responsibility for ensuring their realization. Even in the United Kingdom, with its apparent determination to avoid a Bill of

Rights and its public concern at judicialising rights, the rule of law has traditionally granted to the courts considerable powers to ensure, for example, that 'natural justice' is upheld. Judges have, on occasions, taken sides with the underdog against the powerful, for instance in upholding the right to be heard in a legal proceeding, without which natural justice would have been deemed to have been absent.

As the concern for individual rights has become greater in recent years, the importance of courts has also been enhanced. This is true on both sides of the Atlantic. But there are important distinctions. In the .United States, the Constitution is the Supreme Law and contains a number of provisions designed to protect individuals against the overweening or discriminatory power of the state, and the courts adjudicate when claims are disputed, if necessary striking down a law (say, the Arkansas one forbidding the teaching of Darwinian evolutionary theories in school) as unconstitutional. In the United Kingdom, the principle of parliamentary sovereignty ensures that there is no superior law, that even the common law can be subverted if a majority of Parliament so ordain it. Or, at least, that is the dominant conventional wisdom. Recently, however, some scholars and even a High Court judge have suggested that there are some protections for individuals that even a majority in Parliament could not remove. That is still to be tested.

All states need some people to make the laws, to perform, as we might say, the function of rule making. Furthermore, all states need people to put those laws into practice, to perform, as we might say, the function of rule application. Finally, all states need some people to arbitrate between rulers and ruled or between different understandings of the permissible reach of powers granted to servants of the state, to perform, as we might say, the function of rule adjudication. It is this final function that I wish to explore.

The Importance of Individual Judges

Before peeling off the complexities of judges' involvement in political activity, like the skin of an onion, it is essential to explain why I want to focus explicitly on judges in addition to the judiciary as an institution that is part of the whole governmental system, or judicial philosophies as ways of resolving disputes brought to the courts. The judges themselves must lie at the heart of any examination of a judicial system. And the reason for this is as important as it is central. While judges do often agree among themselves, they also disagree. In the United States Supreme Court, slightly less than 30 per cent of the cases heard are decided unanimously and even then the reasoning behind the agreed outcome may be diverse. In the Judicial Committee of the House of Lords the figure is more like 70 per cent. In the civil law traditions of Germany and France, initial determination to produce unanimous decisions as symbols of the objective certainty of the law has only recently given way to an acceptance of dissents and disagreements.

The truth of the matter is that able judges disagree over hard cases and much of the docket of the highest courts – the courts of last resort, as they are called – are indeed hard cases. Lord Reid once expressed the indeterminacy of much of the British common law in these delightful words: 'Those with a taste for fairytales seem to have thought that there is some Aladdin's cave where is hidden the Common Law in all its splendour and that on a judge's appointment there descends on him knowledge of the magic words Open Sesame. Bad decisions are given when the judge has muddled the password and the wrong door opens. But we do not believe a fairytale any more'. To make this more explicit, consider briefly the success of Mrs Gillick's attempt to prevent a doctor prescribing contraception to her fifteen-year-old daughter. In the High Court, before a single judge, she lost her case. The Court of Appeals reversed by 3 to 0. In the judicial Committee of the House of Lords that decision was itself reversed by 3 to 2, thus handing Mrs Gillick defeat even though five of the nine judges to hear her case agreed with her.

Take, as another example, a woman's right to an abortion in the United States. In 1973, seven of the nine Justices accepted in *Roe v. Wade* that the constitutional right to privacy was broad enough to encompass a woman's absolute right, in the first trimester of her pregnancy, to decide, in consultation with her physician, whether or not to carry a fetus to term. In 1983, this absolute right was reaffirmed in *Akron v. Akron Reproductive Services,* but now by six votes to three, Sandra Day O'Connor having replaced Potter Stewart. In 1985, the majority upholding a woman's fundamental right to an abortion in the first trimester was reduced to one, when Chief Justice Warren Burger left the majority in *Thornburgh v. Gynaecologists and Obstetricians.* Then, in 1987, after Antonin Scalia had replaced Warren Burger and Anthony Kennedy had replaced Lewis Powell, *Webster v. Reproductive Services* cut back the right without actually removing it, with four Justices apparently prepared to reverse *Roe* entirely. And in 1989, in *Casey v. Planned Parenthood of South-East Pennsylvania*, a very divided Court reaffirmed the right to an abortion set out in *Roe*, but also permitted considerable regulation of that right, even in the first trimester. Two Justices wished to keep the woman's right to choose absolute; four Justices wanted either to remove the constitutional basis for the right altogether or to leave regulation entirely to state governments without oversight by the federal courts; three

Justices wanted the right to have constitutional protection, but wanted also to permit states to regulate abortions throughout the period of pregnancy so long as they did not impose 'an undue burden' on the woman.

There is no doubt that changing Justices can mean changing the law, although, as I shall discuss in the next chapter, this certainly does not mean that judging is entirely personal and unprincipled. Nevertheless, it is easy to see how important a new judge or justice can be to a collegiate court. This is spectacularly clear if I describe a famous and recent occasion when the nomination of a single person to the Supreme Court of the United States sparked one of the most passionate moments of recent American history. In the United States, there is no escaping from the fact that the politically aware attach enormous importance to judicial appointments. Each new nomination to the Supreme Court is a subject of intense interest to the politically involved.

In 1987 Justice Lewis Powell, the courtly Virginian, approaching his eighty-fifth birthday, decided to retire from the Supreme Court. Liberal interest groups had feared precisely this eventuality. Powell, although in many ways a conservative in his generally supportive position towards duly constituted governments, their officials and the law enforcement officers, had nevertheless cast several liberal votes in many of the closely divided 5–4 decisions that had upheld the constitutional right to an abortion, the propriety of carefully crafted affirmative action programmes, and a stout wall of separation between church and state. If he were to be replaced by a Justice who interpreted the Constitution differently, the right to an abortion would be annulled, the principle of affirmative action programmes discarded, and the division between church and state compromised.

President Reagan nominated Judge Robert Bork to take Powell's place. At first sight, Bork was an ideal candidate. He had been a law professor; he had been the nation's solicitor-general (who argues many cases before the Supreme Court) in Nixon's presidency; he had experience as a judge on the Washington DC Circuit Court of Appeals. But there was more to Bork than that. He was an activist and a propagandist, the idol of the committed right and the symbol of revived conservatism in the 1980s. He felt that *Roe* had been wrongly decided, that affirmative action programmes were contrary to both the Civil Rights Act of 1964 and the Fourteenth Amendment's requirement that no state should deprive anybody within their jurisdiction of 'the equal protection of the laws', and that the Constitution did not command a wall of separation between church and state. In contrast to Powell, he had taken considerable pride in making his positions clear in lectures and speeches across the country. He was a lightning rod. It was exactly this confident espousal of conservative positions that endeared him so much to the activists of the right, to whom Reagan owed a debt of gratitude, and at the same time made him a demonic figure to the left, who were smarting under the conservative revolution begun by the Reagan Administration. The nomination, as one of Bork's most determined supporters put it to me, was about the soul of American culture.

Hyperbole of this kind rang strongly on both sides of the political divide. Senator Edward Kennedy, well primed and genuinely appalled by the prospect of a Justice Bork, was ready with a powerful, damning and headline catching diatribe immediately Reagan's choice was made public. 'Bork's America', he told the television interviewers, 'is a land in which women would be forced into back alley abortions, blacks would sit at segregated lunch counters, rogue police could break down citizens' doors in midnight raids, school children could not be taught about evolution, writers and artists could be censored at the whim of the government, and the doors of the federal courts would be shut on the fingers of millions of citizens for whom the judiciary is – and is often the only – protector of the individual rights that are the heart of our democracy'. It was unfair, overstated and outrageous, but it caught the mood of a host of organizations desperate to prevent Bork casting what they feared would be decisive fifth votes to cut back and destroy what they conceived to be the great victories won in the courts over the previous quarter of a century. They raised large quantities of money; they bought airtime to beam negative advertisements, including one with a Gregory Peck voice over; they lobbied Senators mercilessly in their home states; they co-ordinated their propaganda and meticulously utilized the opportunities offered to supporters on the op-ed pages of the newspapers. In short, they ran a campaign as though Bork was running for elective office.

He was doing nothing of the sort. Indeed, the process for filling vacancies on the Supreme Court was designed by the Constitution's Founding Fathers in 1787 precisely to ensure that such positions did not become the subject of open partisan battle. The formal procedures for filling a vacancy on the Supreme Court involve only a handful of people. It is the president's prerogative to nominate a person of his choice. Normally, he would consult with his closest advisers, especially his attorney-general or, perhaps, the White House counsel. He would also be bombarded with suggestions from a raft of interested parties to whom he perhaps owed some kind of political debt and he would keep a weather eye open to the political possibilities of a strategic nomination. Ironically, Bork had not been nominated in 1986 partly because the alternative candidate, Antonin Scalia, was an Italian-American, from which community no Supreme Court

Justice had yet been drawn, and Reagan felt that such a nomination would strengthen his position electorally among the Italian-American community. The nomination is then passed to the Senate Judiciary Committee, which holds more or less extensive hearings as its chairman organizes, before a recommendation is put to the full Senate to vote on. Constitutionally, the Senate must advise and consent to each nomination, but history has expunged the advisory role and left merely the consenting responsibility. But it is the task of the Senate, already having been elected, to make the final judgement on whether a presidential nominee should be confirmed or not and one such nomination in five has failed to receive this blessing. In Bork's case, the Senators learned full well what their electors felt, what their natural political allies wanted, and what the academy and elite Washington thought. The detailed nature of Bork's qualifications gradually diminished in importance as the political fallout from voting one way or another came home to the individual Senators. He was voted down 54–46.

This may be thought of as just another example of American exceptionalism, eccentricity or what you will. Certainly, the British system has no parallels. Appointments to the High Court and to the Judicial Committee of the House of Lords receive remarkably little attention, even when the choice is clearly going to have some significance (such as bringing the British representative on the European Court in Luxembourg back to London). There is no examination of candidates by the legislature; rather, the Lord Chancellor or the Prime Minister, on his recommendation and after unpublicized soundings, merely announce the new appointments. Nor do the press take time, space and trouble to comment on the possible significance of new appointments. In part, of course, this is because the fairytale to which Lord Reid referred is still widely protected and there would seem to be something improper in even suggesting that a new member of the High Court or the Judicial Committee would act in any way other than in the 'correct' way that the best and most skilled of lawyers, through their specialist expertise, can achieve.

When Lord Chief Justice Taylor announced his retirement in the spring of 1996, the broadsheets briefly focused upon his tenure and the changes consequent upon his decision. The successor's name was soon leaked to the appropriate journalists and there was virtually no discussion, either in the press or on the television or in Parliament itself, about a range of possible candidates for so important a state position. Quietly, secretly and efficiently, the internal procedures operated as usual and an important and controversial post was filled with little or no public debate or evidence of public concern. In fact, the appointment should have provoked considerable interest and comment, because not only did Sir Thomas Bingham have a reputation as a modernizer and reformer but his elevation opened up the position of Master of the Rolls to which Lord Woolf, a well known activist on most conservative critics' black list of judges, was – with equally smooth despatch – appointed. Such important changes only momentarily diverted attention from other matters and different agendas that tend to dominate editors' priorities; they reflected beautifully the culture not only of privacy but also of the non-political nature of judicial positions which dominates in Britain.

Elsewhere, judicial appointments are much more often seen for what they are. They can certainly ruffle the political equilibrium. In 1994, in the Republic of Ireland, prime minister Albert Reynolds nominated to the Appeals Court a man whose past so antagonized one of the partners in his coalition government that he was obliged to resign and, after several days of doubt and hesitation, a new government with a new prime minister was formed. At the end of the same year, an ailing Francois Mitterrand – unpopular and close to the end of his term of office – used his prerogative to appoint three old colleagues and political affiliates to the *Conseil Constitutionel* in the hope that his vision of how the French Constitution should be interpreted would outlast his own occupancy of the Elysee Palace.

Different countries have different procedures for selecting their most senior judges. In most, there is a high degree of involvement by active politicians and the chief executives take a keen interest in who is chosen. Active engagement in the political arena used to be a common prerequisite for a senior judgeship in the United Kingdom, but it is very much less so now (although many of the senior judges have been politically active in their early adult years). In the United States, especially under Democratic Party presidents, political service was most common and that service could be at a very high level; Howard Taft had actually been President before becoming Chief Justice! In France, too, in direct contrast to its system of formal career patterns for judges in virtually every other national court, from post-university training through to a seat on the *Court de Cassation* for the very brightest and luckiest, appointments to the *Conseil Constitutionel* are highly political. The reasons for this are at least twofold. In the first place, the hard decisions facing courts of last resort often require the judges to have a feel for the political world and a sense for what would, and would not, be appropriate. As I shall show in the next chapter, there are occasions – not many, perhaps, but important ones – when the judges have felt obliged to consider the political consequences of deciding one way rather than another or requiring one form of remedy rather than another. In the second place, politicians who make the nominations tend to know other politicians well and, in making a judgement about how a possible nominee would perform on the bench, it is natural to turn to a class of public figures whose performances are familiar.

The story of Robert Bork's failed nomination is a special example (and there are plenty more instances, although not so dramatic) that many people think it matters greatly who the judges are. The reason is very simple: different appointees might decide cases differently and thus tilt the balance of advantage to one group of citizens rather than another. This is as true in Britain as it is elsewhere. When newspapers were attempting to publish the disclosures of the MI5 employee Peter Wright, and to publish parts of his book *Spycatcher*, the government was adamant that the law had to be used to prevent any such revelations, and so sought an injunction, a legal instruction forbidding a certain course of action. The courts responded in different ways, depending upon the judges who sat to hear the case. Initially, the first judge to hear the case granted the government its desired injunction, thus preventing the *Sunday Times* publishing excerpts of the work, already on the bookstalls in the United States. The Court of Appeal reversed and Sir Nicholas Browne-Wilkinson (as he then was) maintained that, since the information which the government wished to control was already in the public domain (albeit outside the United Kingdom) there was little purpose in supporting the injunction. On appeal, the Judicial Committee of the House of Lords, in an acrimonious and divided opinion, reinstated the injunction, by three votes to two, on the grounds that nothing final was decided by an injunction and nobody's interests were really harmed so long as a decision on the substance − whether Peter Wright's revelations could be published at all − was speedily dealt with. I think the overall voting was four in favour of an injunction and five against.

It is hardly surprising, then, that politically active groups have an interest in who those judges are and a reason to attempt to influence those in whose gift judgeships lie. It is, therefore, only to be expected that politicians and their supporters should be intimately involved in the processes by which the nations' highest courts are filled. In rule-based, constitutional states those courts will determine, to the benefit of some, how the rules and constitutional provisions will be applied on the ground and, as I have already observed, will effectively exercise power or 'authoritatively allocate values'.

The Difficulty of Judging Hard Cases

Although it is clear that courts must exercise the power of adjudication, it is not clear what principles should, or do, determine the way such power is exercised. The traditional view of the judge's task, along the lines of Lord Reid's fairytale, is formulaic and leaves little, or no, discretion to the judge. In this view, what needs to be accomplished is an examination of the facts in a dispute, relate them to the current laws of the land and the relevant precedents and, consequent upon the skill and learning enjoyed by a senior judge, apply that understanding of the law to the particular case. The job may be well or ill done, depending upon the professional quality of the judge, but the essential, central assumption remains that judging is an activity that can, and should, be separate from any individual's own subjective value judgements. The essence of this view is captured in the famous, and much quoted, words of Justice Owen Roberts, who wrote in *United States v. Butler* in 1936 that the judicial duty was simply 'to lay the Article of the Constitution which is invoked beside the statute which is challenged and to decide whether the latter squares with the former'. I refer to this as the slot machine theory of judging: line up the relevant pieces (facts, law, precedents) and the efficient machine will automatically produce a result however you pull the bandit's one arm. Although the starting point of any judging must be the letter of the law or the Constitution and the precedents that are relevant, this is merely a starting point. In many cases it is also the finishing post. This point should never be forgotten as we explore the minority of cases, but often the most significant cases nationally, where the slot machine cannot cope with the problem before it.

The kinds of cases which reach the highest courts of a country are precisely those where the law is unclear or precedents point in mutually contradictory directions or the facts are unprecedented and there is no clear guidance open for a judge. In these instances, as the great American jurist Oliver Wendell Holmes once put it, the judge is forced to exercise the 'sovereign prerogative of choice'. Such a choice may be firmly grounded in principle, yet still have major political ramifications. Such a choice may carefully consider the consequences of one course of action rather than another, especially the likely political fallout. Such a choice may require the persuasion of other judges or bargaining with other judges to ensure a decision in a collegiate court. These issues form the basis of chapter two.

Since, especially in appeal courts of last resort, the issues are too complex, or too novel, for the 'slot machine' jurisprudence associated with simple visions of the judges' role, it is important to know and understand what values and philosophies generally guide judges. One can feed in neither the facts of the dispute (for their significance and detail are usually contested by the parties) nor the relevant precedents and applicable Acts (for these, too, are not obviously correct or unquestionable) and thereby 'find' the right result. Judges are obliged to make choices and value judgements. For the most part, it has been argued, judges are conservative and consequently, where doubt exists, choose conservative alternatives. As Herbert Marcuse once observed, law and order are always and everywhere 'the law and order which protect the established hierarchy'. Drawn from similar economic and educational backgrounds, they bring a biased set of assumptions, defensive of the *status quo* and normally sympathetic to the interests of property and government itself. Chapter three looks in some detail at this view.

Implicit in virtually all the commonsensical and bar room argumentation over the performance of judges are two unspoken assumptions. The first presumes that judging is a special skill, qualitatively different from that needed and exercised by a politician, and that it stands in some way intrinsically opposed to the political. I accept that view, with a single, but essential, caveat: while judging and politicking are different, the consequences of the two activities may often have much in common. The second assumption, at least, is that the decisions that affect our lives, whether through acts of commission or omission, should be made by politicians. The sovereignty of Parliament, the idea that the ultimate source of legitimate power can only be the Parliament whose members we have elected, is paramount. I do not accept this view, partly because I believe it to be misplaced in theory and partly because it does not achieve the purposes of the state. These issues are addressed in chapter four.

What I have tried to show in this introductory chapter are three things. First, in any system of government (and this is as true of the traditional societies of tropical Africa or the former communist regimes of Eastern Europe as it is true of the liberal democracies), there is a need for people to make authoritative decisions over the meaning of constitutional provisions and legislative wording. We call these people judges. They are necessities. Second, this task is not merely a technical job with little or no ramifications for the inhabitants of a state, such as weights and measures inspectors might carry out, but a job where there are alternative possible responses and thus different outcomes. Consequently, who the judges are and how they are chosen is a matter of significance for all of us.

2

JUDGES AS POLITICAL ANIMALS

All governments seem to perform three quite distinguishable functions. These are generally referred to as legislative, executive and judicial. In essence, the legislative function is concerned with discussing and promulgating laws, what might be termed rule (or law) making; the executive function is concerned with administering those laws, what might be termed rule application; the judicial function is concerned with disputes that arise under the laws, whether, for example a law has actually been broken or what a particular clause in a law really means, what might be termed rule adjudication. It is important to be quite clear about the central function of the judiciary, which is essentially responsive, 'a substantially passive instrument, to be moved only by the initiative of litigants', as the American Supreme Court Justice Robert Jackson once expressed it. While the consequences of judicial decisions may be far-reaching, the judges' position in the political order is clearly after the legislature has made the laws and the executive has applied (or threatened to apply) them. Judges are therefore quite different from politicians.

Politicians, by contrast, openly seek access to state power and are primarily initiating and making the laws to advance their own or their supporters' vision of what the state's government should be doing. They have a purposive function to advance public policy proposals in whatever area of life they think appropriate in a democracy, to seek support for them from the citizenry and to translate them into law, binding upon the inhabitants of that state.

They are movers and shakers. They are partial, committed, goal-oriented. They are, moreover, the means in a modern polity by which popular demands are transmitted to governmental structures and then acted upon. In many countries, they receive a poor press and the level of disillusionment with them is disquietingly high. For democracies can only function well if the transmission belt between the governed and those exercising the authority of the state, that is the politicians, works efficiently and with the support of the citizenry.

Members of the judiciary, by contrast, are held to operate in a very different milieu, indeed, one strikingly opposite to the politicians' in many ways. They wait upon others to generate disputes and bring them to the courts. They are limited by the nature of the cases before them as to the issues of public policy with which they get involved. They are bound by procedures and past decisions, and their function is to arbitrate neutrally between parties according to the procedures, laws and precedents others have crafted for them. Initiative plays second fiddle to reaction. When critics claim that judges are 'political', they are not only making an empirical statement, describing what judges do, but a normative statement, implying that judges have strayed from their proper path into the domain of others.

Although in practice, as we shall see, this summary of the judicial branch's role in the state leaves a great deal unclear and questionable, it is essential to distinguish sharply between the political, which is the proper sphere of the politician (in the liberal democracies armed with the legitimacy of popular elections), and the judicial, which is the proper sphere of the judge, whose position rarely depends upon elections or periodic renewal of its mandate from the electorate. Neither remains confined entirely to their own sphere. There is, indeed, overlap, but a fundamental difference nevertheless remains. It is a difference that is virtually absolute in normative terms, but only relative in empirical terms. What we see, especially in the United Kingdom, is a remarkable public commitment to the idealized model. Judges naturally hold it firmly; they have an interest in so doing. But politicians in power can also with equanimity assert their confidence in the impartiality and neutrality of the senior judges, especially when they have found in the government's favour. When the Law Lords upheld the complaint against the Greater London Council for setting up a fare structure that required additional financial support from the ratepayers of boroughs within the Council's jurisdiction, Labour MPs complained bitterly that the judges were acting politically. The judges, claimed Alex Lyon in the House of Commons, 'were making political decisions and not judicial decisions'. Not at all, was Mrs Thatcher's reply: 'I wholly reject that', she said. 'Judges give decisions on the law and on the evidence before them. They do so totally impartially'. For the Labour MP, the accusation was both empirical (the judges *had* decided according to political rather than judicial principles) and normative (judges should not act in this manner). For Mrs Thatcher, the normative point need not be addressed, but was implicitly accepted, because the empirical judgement was waved away as entirely without foundation.

This chapter tries to untangle the confusion over what it could mean to assert that judges are behaving politically and also, which is no less important, over whether judges should ever behave politically. As will be seen, judges must on some occasions behave politically, and would be wise on others to behave politically, yet should not, in another sense of the word, ever behave politically! To sort out this obvious contradiction, we must consider what it might mean to say that a judge is acting politically.

It may seem rather perverse to devote a whole chapter to judges as political animals, when it is part of nearly every nation's accepted political mythology that judges should not be political animals. An easy justification is the fact that criticism of judges is often couched in terms implying that they have improperly strayed from their separate field – rule adjudication – into the field set aside for legislative politicians, namely law making. But there is another justification. When we say that somebody is political, whether we are referring to a judge or a friend, a colleague or an entrepreneur, we mean to convey something of significance. Sometimes, the message is merely an empirical observation of what actually happens, but more often the message is a normative statement about how judges ought to act. The problem is that we can, and do, use the adjective 'political' in very different ways and I believe that there are six distinctive ways in which it can be, and is, applied to judges.

Judges are Political by Definition

The first sense of political is somewhat academic, but it is nonetheless central to any evaluation of the relationships between judges and politicians. It revolves around the question that is simple to pose but hard to answer: what is it that makes a particular action political? The response must go back to our conception of the state. This is both a geographical space and also a set of institutions through which the rules that govern the inhabitants of that state are decided. All states contain disagreements; regulating those disagreements is the purpose of politics, hence any procedures and performance that contribute to such regulation are political. For the most part, the rules that govern the relations between the state and the citizen and between the citizens of the state are promulgated by people whom we would instantly recognize as politicians. They might be individuals who seek that authority through the process of elections, or they might be individuals who seize the powers of the state by military force or internal insurrections. In either case, we recognize without difficulty that these individuals are openly and systematically seeking to acquire the powers of the state in order to enforce upon the population of the country the values or policies that they prefer.

The dominant players in this game are definitely politicians. But it is also the case that some decisions are made by judges. For the most part, as we shall see, judges give their blessing to the rules that the recognized politicians have agreed upon. However, there are occasions, not very many in all but usually very visible, where judges decide that those in authority have overstretched their legitimate powers or have acted in a away that is forbidden by law. Their decisions have the same impact, the same form or consequence, as if they had been made by the politicians. To that extent they are political, whether the judges like it or not. This is a definitional matter. If we recognize that the purpose of politics is to decide upon a set of values (all policies are essentially normative in their subjectivity) that have the authority of the state behind them and are therefore binding upon the state's inhabitants, whoever (or whatever institution) makes these decisions is political. Courts are, therefore, often political. We should not be carried away by this simple truth into believing that courts are nothing but political institutions; that would be absurd. Most of what courts do is not about authoritatively allocating values across the state but about dealing with a specific complaint or disagreement between two parties, often private individuals or corporations. But, when the issue at hand is a matter of public concern and public applicability, then the decision of the court is necessarily political. Whether it upholds a piece of legislation or regulation or executive action, or whether it strikes them down, the end result is political, for that decision will have authoritatively allocated values.

Hence, the first point that needs to be made is a very simple but very important one. Many of the things that courts are called upon to do (evaluating the constitutionality of a government's action, resolving a dispute between a citizen and the state) are by definition political. They allocate rewards or advantages, or take them away, whichever side they support. It was Robert Jackson, again, who put it clearly and succinctly: 'Any decision which confirms, allocates or shifts power as between different branches of the Federal Government or between it and a constituent state is equally political, no matter whether the decision be reached by a legislative or a judicial process'. In this sense of the word, we are concerned with the function or purpose of a public institution − authoritatively to allocate values − and so it is entirely possible that institutions whose *primary* purpose may be something different will nevertheless, in part, contribute quite clearly and explicitly to a task that is presumed rather simplistically to reside in only one place. Let there be no mistake. All courts of last resort are often political, in this definitional sense. But this, of course, is only one of the word's meanings and we need to explore the others.

Judges are Forced to be Political by Litigants
There is a second sense in which courts have become political. They have been dragged into the political process by other activists. This has always been the case in the United States, where culture and tradition have, since the Republic's inception, encouraged its citizens to litigate. As de Tocqueville noted more than 150 years ago, there is scarcely an issue that divides the American people that does not, ultimately, end up in the courts

for resolution. This is a pardonable exaggeration, but it is remarkable how the Supreme Court has, over the last century, struck down segregation in state schools, established a range of suspects' rights, moved towards a constitutional principle of gender equality, instructed executive officers to stop bugging potential subversives or to spend money duly appropriated by the Congress, created – and then cut back – a right to an abortion, briefly dismantled the death penalty regime before sanctioning its successor, struggled with definitions of pornography and principles by which it might be regulated, and found no privacy rights for consenting adults. Had there been more space, the range of policy issues could have been extended to cover not only social policy but also aspects of economic policy and even parts of foreign policy.

In the Anglo-American tradition, as the United States Constitution makes clear, there must be a genuine case or controversy between two parties before the services of the judicial branch may be involved. The adversarial system pits the state against a defendant or a plaintiff against a respondent, each case presenting a dispute that divides the parties and that reflects not a potential but an actual loss to one of the parties. This is still the case, except where waiting until a definable loss has been incurred would render the whole purpose of the litigation void. Hence, claims that the death penalty would be unconstitutionally imposed are heard before the real loss is experienced and claims that limitations on political communication would render an election unfree and unfettered are heard before the election takes place. These are the exceptions. Read the cases that come before the Supreme Court and they are presented in a form that continues to pay obeisance to the principle of personal and adversarial conflict. But look behind the title of the cases and the usually squalid facts that have generated the dispute and you will find a bevy of groups and well-financed organizations who have a distinct interest in their outcome. Courts of last resort – and this is as true of the British courts as of the American courts – expend their time and energy almost exclusively on disputes that have a potentially general application and raise principled questions whose resolution will affect many other people and many similar types of dispute.

It is precisely because these cases have a general application that more than the two parties involved have a real interest in the resolution of the dispute. In the United States, there has developed over time a practice that enables people who are not parties to a particular piece of litigation to contribute to its resolution by providing to the Court legal arguments or evidentiary data that the actual litigants might not. They do this through filing briefs *amicus curiae* (literally a friend of the Court's brief), and so bring to the Justices' attention much that they might not otherwise see. When the General Electric Company in California was sued by a female employee for not providing maternity benefits, when Californian state law required companies to provide health care for their employees, the alarm bells rang across the United States in those companies who employed a large number of young women of child-bearing age. If pregnancy was interpreted as an illness and therefore required employers to provide sick pay for those 'suffering' therefrom, insurance companies and banks were going to have to budget in the future for many millions of dollars. It was little wonder that a host of organizations other than GEC entered the litigation as *amici curiae* to make their case. The Court probably had a richer presentation of the facts, legal precedents, and likely outcomes than if the GEC lawyers alone had been involved; it certainly had a very much clearer picture of whose 'ox' was likely to be 'gored' and how seriously they were concerned.

The readiness of interest groups and other organizations likely to be affected by the decision in one case to file briefs *amicus curiae* should cause little surprise. If the courts of last resort do, as a matter of fact, authoritatively allocate values, then groups are inevitably going to be very interested in what they do. The United States system makes it possible for interest groups to set up test cases, to support and take on existing cases, and to offer suggestions and information during a case. The most successful of the litigating interest groups has often been held to be the National Association for the Advancement of Colored Peoples (NAACP), whose strategy to undo the constitutional blessing for the principle of 'separate but equal' was vindicated in the *Brown v. Board of Education of Topeka* case in 1954. In the 1950s and 1960s other liberal groups, having failed to advance their political objectives in the legislative arena, turned to the judicial branch. Foremost amongst these was the American Civil Liberties Union, but women's groups were also active and their successes in the early 1970s were in no small part due to the quality of their briefs and the care of their strategies.

By the 1980s, however, conservative groups had also realized, as the business groups had appreciated more than half a century earlier, that it was important to be active in the judicial arena. Supporters of tougher action against suspects and the continuation of the death penalty, organizations devoted to protecting the interests of white males in a legal culture that appeared to permit preferential treatment of non-whites and women, and religious institutions determined to roll back the wall of separation between church and state that the Court had created, all became active as litigators, funders of and advisers to individual litigants, and providers of *amicus* briefs supporting conservative positions. Litigation in the United States thus became just one more part of the interest group pluralism that is both the great virtue of the American system and also its major hindrance.

Interest group litigation is most notoriously an American phenomenon. But it is increasingly being used in the United Kingdom. Test cases are more and more designed to challenge legislation or regulations, and interest groups such as Liberty or the Child Poverty Action Group see litigation as one part, albeit a less than central part, of their overall political strategy. In other countries, such as France, different constitutional and political forces are dominant, but the outcome is oddly similar. Under the 1958 Constitution, bills could be referred to the *Conseil Constitutionel* to check upon their constitutionality. Between 1958 and 1974, when the Gaullists dominated both the legislative and the executive branches, only nine references were made; over the next seven years there were 47, and over the following five years no less than 66. What has happened is that losers in the legislative arena, as in the United States, try and redeem their losses by success in the judicial branch. While this is most obvious in France, it is also noticeable in Germany.

Of course, the increased use of the courts to pursue political goals is noteworthy. But equally noteworthy are two ancillary facts. The first is that litigation is, for virtually all interest groups, the least attractive of options, indeed, a recognition of failure. The vast majority of laws that govern the people in a country continue to be debated and passed by legislatures composed of men and women elected explicitly to do that job. The second fact is that, for the most part, courts uphold the government's laws and administrative actions. They do a great deal more legitimising than they do challenging. Even Mr Howard, if he added up all his victories and all his defeats in the British courts, would end up with a positive score.

I have noted here how interest groups and parliamentarians have brought the courts into the political process quite deliberately. But governments do it as well. When the Conservatives in Britain set up the National Industrial Relations Court, it forced the judges to apply the majesty of the legal process against trade unions in a climate fraught with partisan confrontation. They had few choices, but they were seen by many trades unionists and politicians of the left to be doing the Conservative government's dirty work and not acting as an even-handed and impartial forum in which disputes could be worked through. There was considerable naiveté evident here. Since the very beginning of legislatures, laws have been passed in order to advantage some segments of society and to disadvantage others. Applying these laws, duly passed by partisan majorities according to their words and principles, will inevitably bring the weight of the state down against the losers. The equal protection of the law, as the American Constitution has it, does not mean that every law should treat individuals equally (or how else could differential tax laws ever be constitutional?) but that every law should be applied without fear or favour to the population as a whole. It is thus the obligation of judges, in most cases, to give judgements in such a way that some people are privileged. The political process, through elections, has produced a government whose policies become law and become the authoritative values for the state. Courts must apply them.

So, there really is no way by which courts can avoid being political in this second sense. Their duty is to hear cases that others bring to them and to apply the laws as the legitimate law-makers construct them. What has happened in recent years is that more people have seen litigation as an appropriate way of advancing their own political agendas and more governments have established courts or legal rules that inevitably thrust judges into the heart of the political thicket. Whether this is a sensible way to organize a political system is quite another question. From the perspective of the judge it is a truly academic one, of considerably less significance than the question of how best to deal with the flow of litigation of a public policy (read 'political') nature coming before their courts.

Judges and the Art of the Possible

The third notion of political is a prudential one. I am thinking here of the usage that occurs when we say that a particular course of action would be politic, implying that it would be wise and sensible even if it was not an unyielding application of pure principle. Good conservatives, I suppose, would argue that such behaviour was indeed principled. But there does remain a distinct thread running through criticisms of courts, especially from the legal community, which distinguishes between legal argument, in which judgement about consequences plays a very minor part (let the law take its course) and political argument, which is dominated by calculations of consequences. Hence, any deviation from pure principle, even if the law is made to look an ass or the judgement is unlikely to be heeded, is a derogation from the judicial function. Yet this is by no means a universal view. There is alongside such an absolutist position a view that judges need to consider, on the one hand, the essential justice of an outcome and, on the other hand, the reputation of the institution, which would be impaired if its judgements were met with derision or open disobedience.

Justices are not like nuns – unworldly, cloistered, ignorant of the passions outside, resolutely and consistently principled and answerable only to themselves and their God. Contact with the 'real world', through good relations with their articulate wives and daughters, almost certainly affected the votes of both Potter Stewart and Harry Blackmun in the 1973 *Roe* case. Perhaps the most famous example of justices struggling to accommodate the law with political realities was the process through which the two *Brown* decisions were made. The Court at the time was deeply fractured and its members represented a range of jurisprudential positions, but the final *Brown* decisions were both unanimous. All the members were acutely aware of the likely response, especially in the south, to their decision to announce that the practice of segregation in schools was no longer constitutional, and their deliberations indicate how they tried to square a major policy goal with legal niceties and attempted to fashion a remedy that would be practicable.

Warren was determined that the final opinion should, if at all possible, be unanimous (to emphasize the absolute commitment of a Court well known for its divisions), non-accusatory (to soften the blow of a decision made by nine men, of whom only three could claim to represent the South), simple (to ensure that the widest possible public would read, understand and accept it), and, although clear, nevertheless open to local variations in its application (to encourage a willingness to obey). Consequently, in May 1954 the Court announced the unanimous decision that segregated state schools were unconstitutional and called for argument in the autumn about how this new rule might best be applied. In May 1955 another unanimous decision called upon the states to make a 'good faith' effort to desegregate and to advance 'with all deliberate speed' to the dismantling of their dual systems.

These positions were caused in part by the various positions that the individual Justices took and reflected the best compromise Warren could broker. But it was caused much more significantly by the belief, fostered by the Justices from southern states, that peaceful change would only come if the responsibility for deciding upon the means was left quite explicitly to the southern states and their school boards, supervised by the local district courts, whose judges were drawn from the southern political and legal establishment. Many have argued that these prudential calculations were fruitless. After all, ten years from the time the *Brown* decision was handed down, barely 2 per cent of black children in the deep south went to desegregated schools. By 1969, the Court was finally drawn to announcing that there had been altogether too much deliberation and far too little speed. Yet, it could be argued that the massive resistance that the desegregation decisions sparked off would have been more violent, more intrusive, and more difficult to heal, if the Court's remedial decree had been stronger. We cannot know. That is the eternal difficulty with counterfactuals. Furthermore, the long term cost of a major decision that was openly flouted and not applied might well have resulted in a lowering of the Court's prestige to such an extent that other of its controversial decisions would have also been ignored. Indeed, it is unimaginable that the Warren Court could have revitalized the Bill of Rights in the way it did if its reputation had been dramatically lower and its reputation in tatters as the result of staking out too progressive a position in a country where progressivism does not enjoy naturally fertile ground.

It is essential for the survival of any institution that its decisions should be broadly acceptable to the wider community. The justices, if they have not actually taken a standard introductory political science course setting out the Court's role in the American system of government, know full well that it is part of the governmental structure and that its legitimacy depends upon articulating positions that are at the same time in line with popular opinion and seemingly grounded upon the Constitution. The Court has no instruments of coercion, its judgements are merely pieces of paper and it depends upon its continuing status and the people's and the politicians' readiness to obey. Alexander Hamilton, when recommending the Constitution to the people of New York state for their ratification, took pains to argue that the Court was the 'least dangerous branch' because it had neither the sword nor the purse to back its judgements. All Justices are aware of this. One reason for not reversing the *Roe* decision was that, if the Court did so decide, it would look to the American people (rightly) that the meaning of the Constitution depended entirely upon the individuals who were nominated and confirmed to the Court rather than on any neutral principles greater and more long lasting than the Justices themselves. It is therefore eminently sensible that Justices think hard about the context in which their court is situated and the political environment into which their decisions will fall.

Nobody was more aware of this reality than Harry Blackmun, when the question of the constitutional right to an abortion reached the Court. When decisions are handed down, the author of the Court's opinion normally summarizes in a cursory fashion the finding and basic justification of the decision. In a memorandum to his colleagues, Blackmun reiterated a point he had made at Conference that 'the decision, however made, will probably result in the Court's being severely criticized' and, just before he circulated the final version of his opinion, he sent round another Memorandum that began: 'I anticipate the headlines that will be produced over the country when the abortion decisions are announced', and he enclosed a copy of the statement he had carefully crafted to explain precisely what the findings of the Court were in the hope that 'there should be at least some reason for the press not going all the way off the deep end'. His hopes were initially fulfilled, but not because of his carefully considered briefing for the press. Lyndon Johnson died on the same day that *Roe* was handed down and the ex-president dominated the newspapers for the next few days. It was only later that the full import of Roe was appreciated and then, as Blackmun had feared, it was simplified into a manichean struggle between the pro-choice forces defending a woman's absolute right to an abortion and the pro-life forces who saw every abortion as the murder of an innocent fetus.

There are, of course, different views on what a prudential course of action might be. Antonin Scalia, for example, has publicly argued that the Court's involvement in the abortion controversy is against the Court's interests. 'Leaving this matter to the political process', he wrote, 'is not only legally correct, it is pragmatically so. That alone – and not lawyerly dissection of federal judicial precedents – can produce compromises satisfying a sufficient mass of the electorate that this deeply felt issue will cease distorting the remainder of the democratic process.' Scalia's prudential calculations extended a stage beyond a legalistic worry about how an opinion would be received in the wider community to the consequences for the institution itself. Once a court accepts that it is competent to make a resolution of a disputed issue, it must be prepared to receive the accolades and, more uncomfortably, the brickbats that come with success and failure respectively. The *Brown* decisions, although initially criticized rightly for their jurisprudential weaknesses and political goals packaged as legal theory, have come, forty years later, to be accepted as two of the most important, and most praiseworthy, in the Court's history. The abortion decisions have not received such positive acclaim. While individual women will come up to Harry Blackmun and thank him tearfully and emotionally for the courage of his convictions, a large and vocal minority look upon the *Roe* decision as an invitation to murder. If the substantial majority of the Court that found that a woman's privacy right was broad enough to encompass the decision whether or not to carry a fetus to term had been able to see the picketing and bombing of abortion clinics, and the assassinations of doctors undertaking abortions, they might have been less enthusiastic about their decision. But 1973 was a very different time from 1993. The women's movement was at its zenith and gender equalities were becoming conventionally accepted among the chattering classes of the east and west coasts, just as there existed the expectation, soon to be dashed, that the Equal Rights Amendment would be passed. Prudential calculation and current opinion run hand-in-hand, as the ebb and flow of the abortion cases indicates. The arrow of the unadulterated law, impervious to such winds, flies unflinchingly straight. There is much to be said for the prudential judge in the real world, even if academics and conviction politicians see it otherwise.

In countries where the executive is less inclined to permit its behaviour to be challenged in the courts and struck down by activist judges, the judges also tend to read the runes and develop a set of jurisprudential rules that lead to conclusions that will be acceptable to the powers of the day. Theories about constitutional evolution, about the law needing to keep abreast of contemporary mores, about the judges requirement to match interpretation with contemporary values are widespread. They will be found in France and in the European Courts, where the European Convention on Human Rights develops its meaning most obviously and naturally through litigation but also through a recasting of existing precedents in the light of changing values in the wider world. Calculating what will be accepted is one part of a judge's job, and since judges tend to reflect the changing values of the establishment from which they are drawn, rights and liberties get redefined pragmatically, prudentially over time.

This is true of the United Kingdom as well. As in the United States, most disputes do not call for such judgement, yet those cases that touch a raw nerve or speak to strongly held, but strongly challenged, beliefs are normally subject to a good deal of prudential calculation. For example, the case of *Heaton's Transport v. TGWU* was treated with special care and attention. As Lord Reid later said, 'You see, you have to take public opinion and public policy into account and that [decision] was for consumption by non-lawyers and it might have been confusing'. A more obvious instance of prudential politics is hard to describe. That, however, was only part of the story, for the decision in the case was handed down with almost unprecedented speed, only a week elapsing between the end of the hearing and Lord Wilberforce's speech. The reason for this was almost certainly a matter of political calculation, for it allowed the National Industrial Relations Court, which had committed dockers to prison for flagrant contempt of court and thus fuelled a movement towards a general strike, to exercise some nifty judicial footwork and, on the strength of the *Heaton's Transport* decision, release the dockers and defuse a difficult situation. The same could be said of cases involving abortion and sterilization, and even issues ruled upon by the European Courts. The thoughtful judge is always calculating consequences in the political arena.

Judges and Power within the Court

We come now to a fourth sense in which courts may be political. The starting point here is the acceptance that judges are normally influence seeking, in the sense that they have a natural desire to prevail in arguments within their court. Courts of Appeal, or courts of last resort, are normally collegiate courts. Courts of first instance, where a case begins its life, tend to take place with a single judge, sometimes with a jury in addition, sometimes sitting alone. But later stages involve more judges. In the United Kingdom, it is normal for a panel of five Law Lords, drawn from the full Committee, to hear a case. Occasionally, that number might be increased, as it was in when a major new principle about how laws were to be interpreted was discussed.

One of the most significant recent examples of a larger panel was the seven-judge panel that considered *Pepper v. Hart* in 1992. At first sight, the question appeared relatively trivial. Should a schoolmaster at an independent fee-paying school, whose child was educated at the school but at an appreciably lower fee than other parents paid (on the presumption that such a child was marginal to the school's overall costs), be taxed on the basis of the full fee, as would any other parent, or on the basis of his lower fee? While the facts did indeed concern just such an issue, the principle at stake was substantially greater. Historically, the Law Lords had interpreted statutes according to their plain meaning and had thought it inappropriate to enquire into the purposes legislators may have entertained when proposing or supporting the Act. On the other side of the Atlantic, by contrast, congressional intention was a central weapon in the arsenal of most appellate court judges. In the late 1980s, just as *Pepper v. Hart* was being considered in the British courts, Justice Antonin Scalia was making some headway in persuading his colleagues to dispense with agonising over congressional 'intention' (which he felt was neither singular nor even knowable) and embrace the British tradition of plain meaning.

The Civil Rights Act of 1964, and its subsequent amendments, was a particular source of friction. In places, the words appear quite clear; discrimination on grounds of race (or gender) was impermissible within all organizations that received financial benefits from the federal government. But a majority of the Court, to the rage of Justices such as William Rehnquist and Antonin Scalia, consistently argued that the intention of this provision was to assist Afro-Americans and women by outlawing practices that would discriminate against their interests. This implied that laws and regulations that worked to advance their interests and make good the consequences of years of prior discrimination could not have been intended by the law-makers to fall foul of these provisions within the Civil Rights Act. Hence, affirmative action programmes that helped Afro-Americans and women, but by definition discriminated against white men, should be upheld. The plain meaning of the Act was rejected in favour of the presumed intentions of Congress.

Ironically, at precisely the moment that the US Supreme Court was moving towards the British tradition, the Judicial Committee of the House of Lords was moving in the opposite direction. In *Pepper v. Hart* the plaintiff, notwithstanding the clear words of the Act, maintained that the progenitors of the Act had a quite different intention for the Bill than the one advanced by the Inland Revenue. The minister had actually said on the floor of the House of Commons that teachers would be treated as receiving only a small benefit and would thus be taxed lightly. The Law Lords used this dispute as a vehicle for considering whether, when applying a statute, judges should remain faithful only to the *words* of the Act or to the clear intention of the Act's progenitors. Against the precedents, they decided in favour of the schoolmaster and hence established a quite new relationship between judges and politicians. It was probably important that so major a change in the principle of judging was taken by a larger panel (over half the Judicial Committee at least) than is usual.

In the United States, all nine members of the Supreme Court hear every case unless a Justice excuses herself or himself because of some connection with the parties involved. This may be because a Justice once acted for one of the parties or worked in the office of one of the attorneys or was a politician in the jurisdiction concerned in the case. The convention is that a Justice can only participate in the final disposition of the case if he or she has heard the oral argument and read the briefs. Oral argument takes up little time, usually a single hour, so few argued cases do not see the full Court on the bench to hear the attorneys present their cases and to question them sharply. After the oral argument, there is a Conference at which the cases argued in the week are discussed and positions taken. The time for persuading colleagues is short and rarely effective; oral argument is one place where Justices' questions can suggest to their Brethren how a case ought to be decided, while the writing of Memoranda and draft opinions is the other. Although collegiate in form, the Supreme Court is, in reality, nine little law firms and it takes a determined Justice to argue and bargain in order to advance a particular legal view. They do so, however; and some are very much better at it than others.

In the United Kingdom, each Law Lord delivers a speech of his own, although increasingly one will make the major statement setting out the judgement and the reasons for it and the others will either signify their approval, or add a few further observations. On occasions, there will be disagreement, and a dissent will be expressed. In the United States, a single member is given the responsibility by the Chief Justice to write an opinion expressing the institutional view of the Court. Alongside that opinion, 'for the Court', there may be several others, concurring opinions, dissenting opinions, even opinions that concur in part and dissent in part. I mentioned earlier the last major case involving the constitutionality of regulations limiting the unfettered right of a woman to have an abortion, when the Court split in effect into three blocs, none of which was a clear majority. Some of the Pennsylvania regulations were upheld (by 7 votes to 2), while others were struck down (by 5 votes to 4), in each case the triumvirate of Justices O'Connor, Kennedy and Souter being in the majority.

Perhaps more remarkable was the crucial case that became the first occasion on which the Court faced square-on the constitutionality and legality of affirmative action. At issue were the procedures for entry to the medical school on the Davis campus of the University of California. Of 100 places, 16 were set aside for minorities. Allan Bakke, a mature white family man, decided in his early 30s that he wished to become a doctor, passed the necessary preconditional examinations and applied for entry. His scores were sufficient at the margin to allow him entry to the 84 open places, but the admission officers decided against him, mainly because the investment in a man of his age would be less cost-effective in terms of years of practice than investing in a younger person. Bakke's scores were better than those admitted on the special programme, but, because he was white, he was ineligible. He sued the University on the grounds that his legal rights under the 1964 Civil Rights Act and his constitutional rights under the Fourteenth Amendment had been abridged.

Four Justices went no further than the Civil Rights Act and argued that his rejection was illegal, since he had clearly been excluded because of his race. Four Justices, to the contrary, argued that both the Civil Rights Act and the Fourteenth Amendment had been intended to assist black (and other minority) Americans to escape from the inferior positions caused by discrimination and it would, therefore, be absurd to strike down a programme that was designed to advance black Americans by using the very Act and constitutional provision introduced to advance them. The ninth Justice was Lewis Powell. He joined the first four in finding that, in this particular instance, the fixed quota used by Davis had indeed denied Bakke his legal rights and that he ought to be admitted to medical school. But he also joined the second four in finding that preferential treatment for minorities was consistent with both the Civil Rights Act and the Constitution, provided that it was just one factor among several involved in making a decision and there were no fixed quotas. Powell's opinion had no supporters for its entirety, but it defined the parameters of affirmative action programmes!

Powell did not find it easy to come to a decision. Each group was keen to bring him unconditionally on to their side, and the gentle Virginian was the recipient of many suggestions and pressures. It seems clear that William Brennan was critical in persuading Powell that he could have his cake and eat it. Brennan knew that Powell not only felt strongly that Bakke had received a raw deal but also that it was essential for the good of the nation that some form of recompense for past discrimination was permitted and, indeed, encouraged. His opinion met both wishes. Brennan was delighted. For him, the broad principle was the critical issue and, if he could create a majority for that, he was content to be in the minority on the particular individual case before the Court. Most cases do not involve the mixture of doubt and influence (where there is no doubt, there is no room for influence), but many cases do.

Disagreements within a collegiate court always occur. How, then, does such a court manage these disagreements? One way is to take no special notice of them and encourage each individual to do their own thing, so that, after every case, a number of opinions are handed down, each reflecting the views of the different authors. Thomas Jefferson encouraged this at the beginning of the nineteenth century, because he was convinced that Chief Justice John Marshall, a long time opponent of his, was corralling his fellow Justices into unanimity against their better judgement and he wanted to see exactly where each member of the Court stood. This is, however, messy and unhelpful. Almost certainly, it will not make clear the overriding principle or principles upon which the case was decided, which clarity would then help lawyers to advise their clients wisely and other citizens to behave within the law, as freshly defined. There is, therefore, an institutional need to attempt to reach a consensus, not only on the particular case – whether to affirm the judgement of the lower court or to reverse it – but also on the rationale. Even the Judicial Committee of the House of Lords has moved in this direction by encouraging one judge to write the lead opinion, to which most of the others will indicate support. In continental systems, it has long been the tradition that opinions should be impersonal and unanimous, thus emphasizing the certainty and logic of the law, rather than its uncertainty and its dependence upon the particular configuration of judges hearing the case.

In all of these systems, there will frequently be some need for discussion and argument. Some people would argue that in these cases judges are, like any other set of participants in an organisation divided over policy, acting politically. They will try and persuade by argument, they will flatter and praise the undecided in order to gain their vote, they will threaten a dissent or a concurring opinion unless changes are made to the opinion of the court and they will cabal with others to achieve their goals. If such behaviour is political, then, indeed, judges on collegial courts are guilty of it.

The best evidence that we have is drawn from the American Supreme Court. That is almost entirely due to the openness of the Justices' private papers and to an academic culture (among legal scholars, political scientists and judicial scholars alike) that believes in judicial biography as a legitimate pursuit likely to throw useful light on the explanations for particular decisions. It is possible, as Alan Paterson has shown, to throw some light on the inner workings of the highest British courts through careful interviewing of judges, but his path-breaking study has, sadly, spawned no major subsequent work. My examples, then, will come almost exclusively from the United States.

In late 1952, the Supreme Court was considering whether the segregated school systems in the United States violated pupils' rights because they denied the children 'the equal protection of the law' mentioned in the Constitution's Fourteenth Amendment, even though, half a century before, the Court had accepted that public facilities could be 'separate but equal', and had effectively used that landmark decision to authorize and legitimate a pattern of segregation that divided the races literally from the cradle in segregated hospitals, to the grave in segregated cemeteries. After the first discussion, the nine members of the Court divided, five in favour – with various degrees of enthusiasm – of affirming the existing principles and four in favour of reversing that precedent and asserting that segregated schools violated the Fourteenth Amendment. But, because the Justices realize how significant their decision would be for the country as a whole, and the southern states in particular, some wanted to take longer over the case, address issues that the parties had glossed over, and return to the case in the next judicial year.

So it was agreed to set the cases over for reargument.

Felix Frankfurter, small, dynamic, confident, politically aware, and Jewish, was probably the most deeply involved and deeply disturbed by the clash between a conventional jurisprudence that required judges to be self-restrained and stand by the precedents, on the one hand, and a belief that segregation was morally objectionable and possibly, but by no means certainly, unconstitutional, on the other. He held little respect for the Chief Justice, Fred Vinson, and despaired, certain that there would be insufficient leadership to reach the right conclusion. In the summer of 1953, however, Vinson suddenly died, prompting Frankfurter to utter the remarkable observation that, for the first time, he recognized that there was a God. Vinson's successor was to be Earl Warren, the former Governor of California, a moderate Republican, and a man with considerable political experience.

The story of how a possible 5–4 division in favour of upholding the 'separate but equal' doctrine shifted to a unanimous decision to strike down that precedent and boldly assert that the Fourteenth Amendment forbade legally segregated schools is a remarkable one. What it shows is the skilful way by which Warren, dealing often with his fellow justices individually in bilateral discussions, step-by-step brought the Court round to an acceptance of his path-breaking position and to a readiness to permit a single opinion to stand for all nine members of the Court. It was Warren's skill as a negotiator, feeling for the position that would maximize support, which he had honed to perfection in his gubernatorial days in Sacramento, that proved so vital.

In 1971, the Court was faced with another issue that divided the

American people deeply. In this case, the issue was whether a court could require a school authority to bus children across its area of responsibility in order to integrate the schools. The new Chief Justice, Warren Earl Burger, decided that the importance of the case required him to author the Court's opinion and he therefore drafted one that was intended to reflect the unanimous decision of the collegiate court to uphold the lower court judge's decree. However, the writing was so unenthusiastic for the principle, so hedged with caveats, so parsimonious as to imply, in effect, the opposite conclusion, that several of his fellow Justices felt unable to sign up to it. Yet, they were politically aware enough to realize that it did matter that the Chief should author a unanimous opinion. So they got together to plan a strategy that would completely alter the final opinion. The group parcelled out parts of the opinion to one another, agreed which sections of Burger's original draft they could live with, and chose as intermediary the Justice least likely to ruffle Burger's temperamental feathers. The opinion in *Swann v. Charlotte-Mecklenburg Board of Education* is a remarkable one and reads like a collage of passages, some of which manifestly have problems of internal consistency. It reads like that because it was a collage. It also illustrates how Justices can, and do, negotiate and bargain, balance their preferences against what is obtainable, and incrementally push the law of the land towards their ideal goal through building coalitions and accepting compromises.

A final example would be another case that has divided the American people deeply from the moment it was decided. Harry Blackmun wrote the Court's opinion in *Roe v. Wade*, but the opinion that was handed down in January 1973 is very different indeed from the draft that he circulated in May of 1972. That draft was criticized from both sides, from the liberal Justices for its failure to engage with the fundamental issue of whether there really was a constitutional right to an abortion, and from the conservative Justices for the weakness of its logic in the face of very recent precedents. Against the vociferous wishes of the most liberal of Justices, William Douglas, the case was held over and reargued in the following judicial term, when two new Justices, both nominated by Richard Nixon, would be able to participate. During the summer, Blackmun worked in the library of the Mayo Clinic in Rochester, where he had been legal counsel before, and his second opinion was very different indeed from the first, addressing the main issue straight on. It was altered in some of its detail at the behest of various members of the majority, but the basic format and argument was undoubtedly Blackmun's. Ironically, the conservatives who had campaigned for reargument in the hope that there might be a majority against creating a right to an abortion were disappointed, and the liberals, who had campaigned against reargument in the fear that there might be a majority against creating a right to an abortion, were rewarded by an opinion more robust and far-reaching than anything Blackmun had considered in the spring of 1972!

By comparison to the United States, the material on the decision-making process in the British courts is, as I have said, fragmentary. Law Lords and Justices of Appeal do not leave their papers to the British Museum Library or to the Rhodes House Archive at Oxford, nor do scholars write biographies of them or devote whole books to the detailed description and analysis of a particular case from its inception through all of its complex legal development to the final judgement and justification. Yet, it is clear from Alan Paterson's work that those involved in any case do not write their opinions or speeches entirely unencumbered by any knowledge of what others are doing or thinking. In virtually all cases, one person becomes the lead author and others embellish the argument, if they see fit. So there is room for some discussion and some attempt to persuade fellow members of the panel to see things one's way. The Judicial Committee is not so collegiate a court as the Supreme Court, where each member of the Court may be involved in every action and case before it, but there may well be a greater likelihood of reaching agreement.

The collegial nature of the Supreme Court can be exaggerated. Influence is nearly always indirect, dependent upon memoranda or law clerk gossip. The Law Lords do act as something more than five independent voices. Discussions, brief and informal though they are, take place throughout the hearing of a case. These are face-to-face and, since arguments in cases are much more extended than in Washington, judges develop together a composite picture of the issues involved and the quality of the arguments before them. The ensuing conference permits those who have taken part in the case to exchange views more formally, and the time spent on the discussion of each case is usually longer than permitted in the Supreme Court's Conference. Speeches are circulated among the participating Law Lords, as in the United States Supreme Court, and sometimes result in amendments to take account of opposing arguments. Only in exceptional cases is much time spent as a body seeking to hammer out an agreed position; unanimity is not valued that highly. But in certain cases, there is no doubt that some Law Lords do attempt to persuade their colleagues, and occasionally succeed. 'Everybody now knows', Lord Wedderburn wrote in 1967, 'that in *Donoghue v. Stevenson* Lord Atkin talked the majority round. It is now generally known that in *Rookes v. Barnard* in 1964 Lord Devlin did much the same'. In this latter case, Devlin was originally in a minority of one (or two, for accounts differ), but, after Lord Reid had reconvened the appellate committee and further argument had been heard, a unanimous decision upholding the appeal finally emerged. There is little doubt that here genuine cases of conversion took place.

The time and care taken in *Rookes v. Barnard* was a sign that the Law Lords realize full well the political significance of the case. Conferences normally last only twenty minutes or so on each case, but occasionally much more time is spent in collegiate discussion. In *Heaton Transport Ltd. v. TGWU*, for instance, a whole day was spent considering the matter, and it was agreed that the Court should take the unusual step of delivering a single speech in order to strengthen the impact of the decision. The search for unanimity almost inevitably demands an interplay of argument and the opportunity for leadership and persuasion on a court. The less concern there is with building majorities, the less need there is for the time-consuming process of persuading colleagues or refining an opinion to encompass a particular argument or line of precedents sought by another member of the majority.

At the heart of the internal politics of a collegiate court is the desire to ensure that an opinion is right, in two senses. It needs to be intellectually right, and the criticisms of colleagues are, in fact, welcomed, since they will help the writer to create a final version that is stronger in its argument and that is ready to mount a counterattack to possible objections once it reaches the public domain. It needs to be politically right in the sense that an opinion for several judges must be tuned to the susceptibilities of those judges. A personal view may make an excellent dissent, but it will fail to keep the majority that writing 'for the Court' requires. Fortunately, few judges or Justices of the Supreme Court have been academic constitutional lawyers brought up on the intellectually exacting demands of law review articles. They have tended to be more practical men and women, politicians who know that the way forward requires a little give and take, or barristers who know that the best arguments are those that persuade the judge and jury rather than those that earn an alpha in the university classroom.

Judges and Political Partisanship
It is only at this stage that I come to the notion of political that dominates common discussion and the media's assumptions. For most people, political implies partisan choices, probably party determined, in which specific policy goals are sought. A political judge starts with the desired outcome, a personal choice, and legitimates his conclusion by devising an argument to uphold the position subsequently, rather than by being led by the logic of legal argument to specific outcomes, as a true judge would do. There is, I think, both a weak and a strong form of this argument.

The weak form argues that judges must, of necessity, have a philosophical position on how judging ought to be carried out and this philosophical position, itself a subjective choice of the individual judge, will have logical consequences of a policy kind. Take, for example, two very different justices of the United States Supreme Court. William Brennan, the son of a trade unionist, a Democrat by familial upbringing and a graduate of Harvard, learned the judicial trade in the courts of urban New Jersey, with its industrial and race problems. On the Supreme Court he developed quickly a vision of the judge's role that reflected his background. Brennan saw the primary tasks of the Court as being to make real the promise of the Bill of Rights and the post-Civil War amendments, and to ensure that the Constitution evolved in tune with the changing values of a maturing society. As a result, he tended to find in favour of individuals who had fallen foul of state regulations, especially where those regulations bore unequally upon people of different races or upon women, and he was prepared to expand the vague phrases of the Constitution, such as 'equal protection' or 'due process' or 'cruel and unusual', to cover behaviour that in earlier decades his predecessors had ignored. Brennan was strongly in favour of affirmative action programmes, deeply opposed to capital punishment, and decidedly supportive of claims to gender equality. His liberal outcomes derived from his first principles. Or, perhaps, those first principles were developed to rationalize the liberal outcomes. There is considerable difficulty in disentangling this causal chain, because the evidence can be cited to support either view.

By contrast, William Rehnquist held staunchly conservative policy views. In the 1950s he publicly criticized the liberal leanings of the Court, where he had himself been a law clerk, and his political friends in Arizona were the close confidants of Barry Goldwater. Brought to Washington by Richard Nixon, he proved himself a deeply conservative, some would say reactionary, head of the office of legal counsel in the Department of Justice. He embraced a judicial philosophy that placed at the top of his values deference to elected politicians and officials, deference to state governments and a belief in the inevitable variability of public policy in a federation, and a conception of the Constitution that sought its meaning, if at all possible, in the intentions of those who wrote it. In his view, the Supreme Court had little business in second guessing elected bodies, had to accept that sovereignty was divided among the several states, and should recognize that there was, in Article V, a proper method of amending the Constitution if the people so wished it. This led him to oppose affirmative action programmes, to support the death penalty, and to refrain from updating the meaning of the Constitution in line with difficult-to-describe changing values.

Committed to a restrained view of the judicial role and a hierarchy of values that put the rights of democratically elected politicians above individual rights, his votes supported conservative outcomes. But his conservative views were well served by such a philosophy.

So, the weak argument would claim that an impartial application of a judicial philosophy is nevertheless policy oriented, because different philosophies will inevitably produce different outcomes. The choice between competing philosophies is subjectively made or, more probably, the unavoidable consequence of a particular individual history. This is entirely to be expected. As I hope I have made abundantly clear, there is no fairytale, no Aladdin's lamp, that makes judging a formulaic exercise. Slot machine theories of justice are, quite simply, unrealistic. In the place of the non-existent guide to all things, a judge must develop a framework, a theory if you like, by which to judge. Since there are many different theories available (and none that is universally accepted as the only legitimate one), judges must choose. That choice will reflect a number of positions: a vision of the purpose of a constitution or the principles of a country's constitutional system; a hierarchy of values when two or more come in to conflict, as they often do; a measure of judgement as to the relative need for the courts by different parties. Put these three positions through the mill of William Brennan and William Rehnquist and you find quite different judicial philosophies. But each man held a set of general principles that guided all but a handful of his votes; in this sense they were both principled. It just happened that their principles took them in different directions.

The strong argument is less forgiving. At its extreme it denies the existence of overarching principles and presumes a simple goal-oriented philosophy, such that judges decide what they think would be good public policy and adjust the flexible means of judging to that end. Some thought that William Douglas, in his later days, operated in this way, deciding what in his view the just result would be and then seeking some kind of support for it. When, for example, he found that a Connecticut law that made the sale and use of contraceptives a criminal offence, he struck it down as an unconstitutional invasion of married persons' right to privacy. Now, the Constitution makes no mention of privacy at all. But Douglas discerned it in the 'penumbra which emanated' from several parts of the Bill of Rights, each of which, by implication, suggested that citizens had a zone of privacy with which governments could not interfere, such as the right to silence, or the right not to have a state religion imposed, or the right not to have militias quartered in the home. This argument seemed to many to be the most overt judicial legislating that could be found. In fact, the legal underpinning of this case was less shaky than the description, commonly held by his opponents, might suggest. Nevertheless, it clearly marked a readiness to stretch the meaning of the Constitution and stretch it in a direction that Douglas felt was right. The thought that police might have to enter the bedroom to check on whether contraceptives were actually being used in order to bring a criminal prosecution was just too much for him to stomach.

This inner feeling of revulsion is clearly evident in a number of decisions made by justices. When the Court was struggling with the meaning of the 'due process' clause of the Fourteenth Amendment, it agreed in the late 1930s that there were some practices that were so unacceptable in a civilized society that they were not congruent with any claim that due process existed. In 1948, Felix Frankfurter, who tended to permit states to legislate largely as they wished, decided that the police practice of pumping out the contents of a man's stomach to disgorge some drugs he had swallowed so outraged the conscience that it could not possibly be associated with due process. It is difficult to get much more subjective than that. Warren Burger was always worried that the *Roe* decision might mean that abortions on demand were constitutionally sanctioned, and he wrote a concurring opinion in the original 1973 case to make it quite clear that this was not the case. In 1985, he decided that a majority of the Court were so interpreting the *Roe* decision, by striking down virtually every form of regulation in the first trimester, that abortions were in effect constitutionally permissible on demand, and so he broke from the majority that upheld the right to an abortion and changed sides. Lewis Powell could write strongly that the right to privacy was broad enough to encompass a woman's right to choose whether or not to terminate a pregnancy, but it was not wide enough to encompass a man's enjoying oral sex with another man. It is said that, only at the last minute, did he change his position and decide to uphold the Georgia sodomy statute.

Carved in marble above the main entry to the Supreme Court are the words 'Equal Justice Under Law' and, if the truth must be told, Justices have on occasions taken this as an invitation to protect what they conceive to be 'justice'. Judges in Britain lack such a ringing declaration of the purpose of the highest courts, but they too have sometimes taken the opportunity to write into the law their own subjective conceptions of right and wrong, justice and injustice. Such opportunities are distinctly rare, but, when issues relating to the provision of contraceptives to under-age girls arise or a health authority's choice not to spend heavily in a specialized area for a single child, the law and precedents are not exactly helpful guides. There are different ways of approaching the problem, some of them very much the sorts of theories, or frameworks for judging, which I have just mentioned. But, in the end, for some of the judges, the ultimate question was a stark normative one: is this the kind of behaviour that I want to sanction or not?

It is difficult to get away from the observable fact that in some situations judges do little more than vote their gut feeling, their subjective policy preferences. But it is important to note two things about such a perception. Only in a very few cases do judges operate in this way. The level of unanimity, in the American courts as well as in the British courts, is high and this suggests either that judges tend to share similar values (to which I will return in the next chapter) or that much judging is a relatively objective task that people of different policy preferences nevertheless agree upon. Second, many of the votes that appear to reflect a personal prejudice are logical extensions of a broad philosophy about the nature of judging and the purpose of the highest courts. As we would expect, humans organize their lives so that their beliefs and their actions mesh together, and it is no surprise, therefore, that judicial philosophy and policy preferences do indeed go hand in hand.

Judges and a Constitutional Dialogue

There is, I think, one other sense in which courts are political. What they do generates responses and actions in the branches of government that are normally thought of as political. Judgements do not die with their birth. They galvanize people into action, journalists into analysis, politicians into criticism, interest groups into action. Lou Fisher has called this process 'constitutional dialogues', because few decisions do not, like a pebble thrown into a pool, create ripples that affect others and demand responses. Again, the American examples are legion. The *Brown* decision was not self-executing, but prompted the school boards in the South to devise all kinds of arrangements to avoid desegregation, required lower courts to adjudicate on a mass of litigation, encouraged the civil rights movement to become more vocal and more active, and ultimately shamed the national government into action in the 1960s. *Roe* had a similar spin-off. Immediately, pro-life groups became more interventionist, state legislatures passed laws and regulations that limited the ease of obtaining abortions, the courts were again required to apply the vague principles of the *Roe* decision to differing sets of facts. The national administration used its resources to support attempts to limit abortions, even to outlaw them.

The same is true in virtually every land. Even though the decision of courts of last resort are supposed to be authoritative and binding judgements that people merely obey, they are rarely the last words on a subject. They are often unclear and need further cases to test their extremities. They normally antagonize some articulate and resourceful people (for, if one side prevails, the other must lose) into trying to circumvent the worst of the consequences. They generate debate and bring home to the judges themselves that there may be weaknesses in their arguments. Even in the systems with the most extreme form of the separation of powers, the political process actually only works if there is some linkage between the functionally separate institutions. As times pass, the personnel on a court change, usually in line with the changing majoritarian view in the capital city, and the communicators either come to terms with the new direction, as happened over segregation in the United States, or continue to challenge it. Judges are not immune to such pressures. They can draw their horns in, revisit a decision or two, and gently bring their jurisprudence more into line with the expectations of the articulate classes.

Constitutional dialogues endure and any examination of judges' involvement in politics must accept that. At the same time, however, it is important to stress that there is a law-making body and law-making procedures through which a nation's statutes are born and developed, and there is an executive branch that administers those laws and uses its discretion to fill in, either by interpretation or by delegated legislation, the gaps left by the law makers themselves. That is the day-to-day truth about government. The courts play their part from time to time, peripherally for the most part, and then only in a small number of areas that, while of great significance to the particular parties involved, are usually of minor importance to the state as a whole. There are exceptions, of course, and the experience of the United States bears eloquent witness to that. But the 'defeats' handed out to Mr Howard are, to be honest, trivial but embarrassing. Their effects outside the narrow confines of public law, however, may be considerable, for they say something about the government and the Home Office that, when translated for popular consumption by the media, may not be electorally helpful. The dance of politics goes on. The judgements of the courts can be part of that fascinating process.

3

JUDGES AGAINST THE PEOPLE

Judges have tended to receive a bad press in history books and at the hands of novelists. Judge Jeffreys remains associated with the Bloody Assizes. The Court of Chancery, as described with evident relish by Charles Dickens in *Bleak House*, was an institution where neither justice nor good sense nor even good manners existed. For Horace Rumpole QC, John Mortimer's fictional barrister, the judges before whom he has to plead appear to be a dyspeptic crew, usually hard of hearing and singularly unconcerned with the due process of the law. Good fiction is always an exaggeration, an enlargement of the foibles of characters and a partial view of reality, but it is recognisable as a comment on the real world. These characters would be cause for derision if it were not the case that they reflected in part the actual state of things.

While judges of the highest courts have been less scandalous in their behaviour than some of their lesser brethren, there are plenty of examples from the past that do not paint the judges in particularly flattering colours. In 1900, a Birmingham journalist took a particular disdain for the presiding judge at the Spring Assizes, finishing his diatribe with these words: 'There is not a journalist in Birmingham who has anything to learn from the impudent man in horsehair, a microcosm of conceit and empty-headedness... One of Mr Justice Darling's biographers states that an eccentric relative left him much money. That misguided testator spoiled a successful bus conductor. Mr Justice Darling would do well to master the duties of his own profession before undertaking the regulation of another'. The journalist was brought before a higher court on the charge of contempt of court and, thanks to a grovelling apology, was punished only by a hefty fine rather than by a spell in gaol. As recently as 1953 a barrister was suspended from practice for four months for 'conduct unbecoming a barrister', when he pointed out that many lawyers, as was true at the time, believed that Lord Chief Justice Goddard was not 'a model of courtesy, fairness and impartiality' when he conducted trials. Since then, the punishment for public criticism of the judges in Britain has reduced, but the readiness to criticize continues in a variety of milieux. The bars round the Law Courts have not changed in this respect, but the fictional presentation of judges on television and in radio plays certainly does not hold them up as complete paragons of virtue. From time to time, too, the tabloid press can launch vicious attacks on individual judges when their editors reckon that some judgement or other is unacceptable. The *Daily Mirror* once had as its front page headline a simple comment: 'You Fools'. This is not the sort of image that judges themselves wish to cultivate.

What is significant is that criticism is generated almost without exception by an individual's dislike of a particular decision, but it is normally couched in a rather different perspective. There is a widespread convention that personal objection to a particular decision is not an adequate basis for a legitimate attack on the courts. Rather, the criticism must be presented in terms of general principle within which a specific decision may rest. It is, then, quite proper to complain that judges have failed to fulfil their appropriate role, but it is cheap to snipe at them merely for adjudicating in an unsatisfactory way.

The principles most often used fall into two categories, which are not mutually contradictory, but which stress two different lines of argument. The commonest is to draw attention to the undemocratic nature of judicial power and to challenge a judgement as a usurpation of the legitimate powers dedicated to elected politicians and their officials, and against the presumed consensus of public opinion. The central thrust of most criticism is that the judges, lacking the democratic basis of electoral support, have overstepped their powers. Hence, the substantive concern is repackaged as a principled, and therefore universal, complaint against a judge's stepping out of line.

The second line of argument stresses the conservative bias of judges and their tendency to support the powerful establishments of a country. Countries differ, of course, but there are few that do not consciously elevate their judges to a status and standing deliberately different from, and superior to, the majority of the citizenry. They may do this by emphasizing the majesty of the surroundings in which courts sit, or by dressing up the judges in finery (much of which can seem absurd), or by giving them honorific titles. Further, the pool from which judges tend to be selected is not a pool that reflects the normal distribution of social backgrounds and abilities, but is an elitist pool of individuals whose contact with, and knowledge of, the lives of ordinary folk may be slim. Although not so direct a criticism as the first, this too suggests that judges may well inevitably be against the people.

Vox Populi

Let us start with Michael Howard's central complaint against the senior judges in Britain. His view was that they were trespassing on the politicians' turf, thus not merely acting in a non-judicial way but, more seriously, in an anti-democratic way. For Howard, the people's voice could only be expressed through elected politicians. Thus, when parliament's leadership decided, in the face of a widespread concern about law and order, that tough mandatory penalties ought to be imposed on those who repeated violent crimes, that decision should be seen as a decision of the people. While judges, as citizens, had every right to express their personal views, judges, as members of the judiciary, had no right to presume that their evaluation of the proposed changes should enjoy any special status. Expertise, or even claimed expertise, had to give way to popular preferences when it came to any authoritative allocation of values.

Michael Howard was not the only person to claim to be representing the people's voice. Most of his political colleagues would want to make a similar claim. In March 1996, a Conservative back-bencher inveighed against a judgement of the European Court in the pages of *The Times*. 'This judge-made law', he wrote, 'enables our domestic courts not only to strike down Acts of Parliament but to override the nationally elected representatives in the country... The British people do not wish to be bound up in the fine arguments that lawyers make... They want a British Parliament to denounce an injustice and not just talk about but to do something'. Others also claim this special relationship to the People; editors of newspapers, especially those running the popular mass circulation variety, have regularly presumed a direct line to the people and asserted that they speak on behalf of ordinary folk. Most rallied behind criticisms of the European Court, asserting with instant confidence that they knew what the British people thought and wanted. This was not new. Most had in earlier days castigated some judges for their public decisions and their private behaviour. For the most part, their wrath had been kept for occasions when sentencing policy had seemed hard to comprehend, nearly always on the grounds that judges had been too lenient. Quick to complain that judges are out of touch, they imply that there ought to be a close correlation between popular policy preferences (or prejudices, if you will) and public action.

It is this view, often more implicit than explicit, that brings together politicians such as Michael Howard and journalists such as Kelvin McKenzie into a populist alliance. At first sight, their position makes good sense. For democratic government is surely about translating popular aspirations and priorities into policies that the full panoply of the state's institutions can administer and enforce. The process by which the originating impulses (the people's views) are converted into outputs (statutes and regulations) involves the election of representatives, the formation of a government reflecting the majority in the legislature, and parliamentary consideration and approval. Politicians have the duty to reflect these views and the newspapers have an obligation to remind all public figures that their democratic duty is to follow those views. The judges should not provide any obstruction to either role. That is, as I shall suggest in the next chapter, a very crude view of democracy, but it has an intuitive appeal and it strikes a ready chord in most people's minds.

Such a populist view favours neither liberal nor conservative causes. Indeed, populism is Janus-like in its ability to look in two apparently different directions simultaneously. One direction embraces the ordinary individual in his or her struggle against the great economic powers of the banks and the monopolies that determine the price of many products, and naturally favours radical policies designed to constrain the economic giants of a country and protect the weaker against the dominant forces of the stronger. The other direction stresses the centrality of

ordinary people's moral views and subjective priorities and tends
to be xenophobic, critical of the unconventional, unforgiving of
the errant, and highly instrumental. The law, and the courts that
administer it, are feared. The suspect and the convicted are
equally resented and felt to be worthy of clear and retributional
punishment; mitigating circumstances are rarely accepted. In this
climate, the politician who favours strict penalties, more
imprisonment, harsh regimes and a stern approach to all criminal
activity finds many kindred souls. Judges who question the value
of strict penalties, believe that custodial sentences have a limited
place in deterring crime, and see in their courts a pitiful array of
incompetent and inadequate individuals alongside determined
and cunning criminals find it harder to discover supporters
among the ordinary folk, who have never studied criminology
or visited prisons. It is not difficult to cast the judges as enemies
of the people.

Constitutional Collisions

Perhaps the most famous political attack on a court for its
undemocratic exercise of judicial power comes from the United
States. In the 1930s, the Wall Street stock market crash and the
ensuing economic depression profoundly affected the US
political scene. The elections of 1932 swept the Republicans out
of power. Apart from Grover Cleveland's presidency 1893-97 and
Woodrow Wilson's presidency of 1913-1921, Republicans had
occupied the White House since the end of the Civil War, and
there had been Republican majorities in the House of
Representatives and in the Senate almost as consistently.
Suddenly, large majorities, made still larger after the 1936
elections, gave Democrats a fresh mandate from the American
people and President Franklin Roosevelt's New Deal programme,
created on the hoof as it were and refined in the face of

experience, ushered in the age of the administrative state. But there were serious doubts as to whether his radical legislative innovations were constitutional. Many believed that they exceeded anything the Constitution had granted the national legislature authority to do. Inevitably, parts of the New Deal were challenged in the courts and the Supreme Court was ultimately called upon to adjudicate.

In a serious of shattering decisions, some unanimous, others with substantial majorities, a few with narrow 5-4 alignments, the legislative (and, to some extent, the executive) response to the crisis of the depression was struck down. This was not an instance of a single rebuff, but a veritable cornucopia of rejections. The Bituminous Coal Act, the National Recovery Act, the Agricultural Adjustment Act, the presidential power to dismiss unsympathetic members of regulatory agencies, all felt the power of the Supreme Court to deprive the electorate of the fruits of their victory at the polls. That, at least, was one cry. The obloquy poured on the Nine Old Men from quarters supportive of Roosevelt's New Deal coalition was strident and telling. It seemed as though the conservative Republicans, whose presidential candidate in 1932, Herbert Hoover, had campaigned firmly against governmental intervention, had achieved their revenge. The Republican appointees had salvaged the ideological soul of American laissez-faire from Democratic attack.

In January 1937, President Roosevelt, with no preliminaries, announced that he planned to ask the Congress to increase the number of Justices on the Supreme Court from nine to fifteen. If this court-packing plan had been passed, the president could have nominated six more Justices, which his massive support in the Senate would have confirmed, and thus almost certainly created a majority to uphold a fresh interpretation of the Constitution and thus to legitimize the new administrative state. Roosevelt claimed, and his more strident supporters shouted in support from the rooftops, that the democratic ideal was being destroyed by the unelected, unaccountable, Justices of the Supreme Court.

It is not difficult to see and appreciate how the conflict between Congress and Court should have been seen in this way. But it fails to take into account several things. Many of the bills were hastily conceived and poorly drafted, some of the government lawyers themselves doubted their constitutionality. In some cases, Acts were struck down unanimously, thus indicating that even those most sympathetic to the president (like Benjamin Cardozo or Louis Brandeis) nevertheless found them an improper exercise of legislative power, and the logic of earlier decisions led the Justices along lines of legal argument that was bound to come into conflict with New Deal legislation. But the political reality of the time and the mythology that has grown up round this episode – a mythology that powerfully influenced academic lawyers as well as judges in the 1940s and 1950s – presents the great cases of 1935 and 1936 as prime examples of judicial power improperly employed, above all to thwart liberal and popular policies. Activism became inextricably associated with conservatism, with the defence of the established forces, with a defiant rejection of a basic principle of democratic government.

As it happened, the clash between Court and Congress did not take place. One conservative Justice retired, to be replaced by a Justice whose view of the Constitution embraced the kind of exercise of power that the emergency had called forth. Another Justice saw, in the second generation of New Deal laws and regulations being challenged, a greater degree of care and direct relationship to specific grants of power in the Constitution and so deemed them constitutional. This 'stitch in time' that 'saved nine' prevented a direct onslaught upon the Supreme Court and reminded the legal community and those concerned with the powers of the judiciary that, in the last analysis, the concerted exercise of power founded upon electoral legitimacy will ultimately prevail. This has not prevented subsequent Courts from striking down some Acts passed by Congress, still less Acts passed by the individual states; but it has been a reminder that at times of major political realignment, courts, reflecting the values and philosophies of a previous political majority, will often appear more obviously anti-democratic.

Something similar happened when the Gaullists, or their centre-right allies, lost the French presidency for the first time since the inception of the Fifth Republic in 1958. Socialists in France bitterly denounced the *Conseil Constitutionel* for its decisions nullifying parts of important socialist legislation in 1982 and 1983. By limiting the nationalisation schemes and the degree of decentralisation proposed, it seemed as though the right were able to block, by referring unliked bills to the *Conseil*, what they had failed to achieve in the National Assembly. One socialist deputy expressed the view that what the Gaullist-dominated *Conseil* had done was a travesty of democracy in these words: 'You are jurisprudentially wrong because you are politically in the minority'. In other words, he was repeating the time-honoured central principle of the French republican tradition that the only legitimate source of state power is the National Assembly, which represents nothing less than the combined wisdom and preferences of the People. The Fifth French Republic, with its new Constitution, was in fact designed by Charles de Gaulle in 1958 precisely to challenge that principle and constrain its consequences. As often happens, losers before courts exaggerate the enormity of what the courts may have done and the political process moves on in response both to the court's action and to the various responses to it. A slightly revised nationalisation bill was adopted within a month of the judgement and upheld by the *Conseil*. The vast majority of bills referred by disappointed minorities were found to be perfectly constitutional, and when the left found itself in the minority, it had no inhibitions about referring bills to the *Conseil* in the hope that the democratically elected majority could be thwarted in the interests of socialist idealism. But that is politics.

As in France, so also in the United States. Both liberals and conservatives use the courts and benefit (or otherwise) from their actions. The crisis of the 1930s pitted the electorally victorious liberals against the judicially entrenched conservatives. But it has not always been like that. In the 1950s, the positions were very much reversed. A liberal Supreme Court began a revolutionary process of imposing upon the fifty states of the Union the limitations introduced for the federal government by the so-called Bill of Rights in 1791. Each year, or so it seemed, the practices of some states, supported by the politicians elected duly through the ballot, were struck down as violative of the Constitution. Segregated schools, and then segregated public institutions of any kind, were the most obvious, but the common practice of requiring verses of the Bible or prayers to God to start the school day were also held to offend the First Amendment's command that there should be no imposition of any specific religion. Then, the Court addressed the practices of the police and the courts and required that suspects be read their constitutional rights (to remain silent, to have a lawyer) and courts to exclude any piece of evidence improperly garnered. After that, the Court turned to the political process itself and struck down the almost universal practice of electing representatives to state assemblies from districts of very variable populations (a whole city like Memphis might elect the same number of representatives as the smallest rural county) and commanded that every vote should be of equal potential value.

These decisions found favour in some quarters, but they also found very determined opposition in others. The complaint, of course, was that the Court had decided a genuine dispute in a way that one of the parties found extremely unattractive. The public voice of that complaint, however, was that the Justices had acted improperly in a general sense and had exceeded their judicial authority by trespassing into the realm of the politicians. Nobody should be seduced by such arguments. There may indeed be a handful of constitutional theorists who do hold that the laws passed by duly elected legislators should trump the limitations of a Constitution. More to the point, many argue that the Justices simply got it wrong and misconstrued the Constitution.

That is a better line of defence, because it allows for later reversal. Here, the United States Supreme Court is perhaps more ready to take initiatives than most other courts of last resort. While it accepts that the principle of *stare decisis* (to stand by the decisions already made or stick to precedents) is fundamental to any system of law, it has also given itself the right to reverse past decisions when they appear no longer rightly decided. The 1896 decision of *Plessy v. Ferguson* first established that, so long as public facilities were 'separate but equal', they did not deny persons within a state's jurisdiction their right to the equal protection of the law. In 1954, a unanimous Court interred *Plessy* when it decided *Brown v. Board of Education of Topeka, Kansas* and asserted that separate schools for black and white children were inherently unequal and therefore automatically violated the equal protection clause of the Fourteenth Amendment. The number of times the Court reverses itself is but a small percentage of all its cases, but it is substantial enough to encourage litigants in their attempts to persuade it quite literally to alter the law.

This, for example, is what many groups, as well as both the Reagan and Bush administrations, tried to do after the Court had asserted, in *Roe v. Wade,* that the right to privacy was broad enough to encompass a woman's decision whether or not to carry a fetus to term. Justice Harry Blackmun's opinion sparked off a determined campaign by Pro-Life groups, as they termed themselves, to reverse that decision. They managed to cut back the fundamental nature of the right and get the Court to accept that states also had rights, when it came to regulating abortions, but they were unable to persuade a majority of the Court to annul the woman's right to an abortion that it had created, with very different personnel, in 1973.

The American experience certainly suggests that, when courts do deny to elected politicians the full fruits of their electoral victories, the cry of anti-democratic goes up, the passions are raised, and the Supreme Court comes in for both verbal criticism and political attack. In the 1950s, attempts were made to pass Constitutional Amendments to reverse some decisions, or to pass legislation that would withdraw from the Court's jurisdiction some areas of controversy, or to impeach the leaders of the liberal majority (especially Earl Warren, but also William Douglas, whose marital arrangements further antagonized his conservative opponents). In the 1980s, the Reagan Administration made a concerted effort to reverse the jurisprudence of the Supreme Court. Not even the Roosevelt years saw so determined an effort to cut back the activism of the Court. The strategy was wide ranging, from taking particular care to nominate to judgeships only those individuals in whom the administration could have real trust, through pressurising the Solicitor-General (who directs and argues the Government's cases before the Justices) to file briefs seeking outright reversal of unliked decisions and supporting Congressional attempts to cut back what the Court had done in the fields of abortion or church and state relations, to launching a scarcely veiled public attack on the Court itself.

Edwin Meese III, Reagan's close friend and second Attorney-General, took the occasion of the annual meeting of the American Bar Association to give a speech that directly challenged the jurisprudence not only of the current Supreme Court but also of the previous Courts back for nigh on sixty years. In another speech, he seemed to suggest that the last word on the meaning of the Constitution need not necessarily be the Court's unique responsibility. Together with a coterie of articulate and conservative lawyers, several Washington think tanks, with their monthly journals and contacts to the media, pressed on with a broad attack on what the Court had been doing for many years. There is nothing particularly liberal or conservative about the sources of criticism of the Court. It depends, as the Americans like to say, on whose 'ox' is 'gored'. In the 1930s, liberals were offended and cried 'foul play'; in the 1950s and 1980s, conservatives were offended and did likewise.

This simple juxtaposition is tremendously important. It is important not merely because it makes clear that antagonism towards the court is a monopoly right enjoyed by neither liberals nor conservatives. It is important because it shows how the dominant philosophy of the Court can change over time, to suit one set of ideas in one period and another set of ideas in another period. The reason for this is simple. Justices are nominated by presidents and confirmed by the Senate. As the political balance in Washington changes, so the basic philosophy of the newly appointed Justices will be different. Successive Democratic presidents, operating with a democratic majority in the Senate, not unnaturally oversaw the appointment of a steady flow of liberal Justices. From the late 1960s, a bifurcated Washington (Republicans in the White House and Democrats dominating the Senate) saw the appointment of basically conservative Justices, as befitted their Republican nominators, but not too conservative justices, as befitted the Democratic majority usually in the Senate. Lewis Powell precisely exemplifies the balance, as did Robert Bork's defeat.

In the end, therefore, the Justices do follow the election returns, or, at any rate, the elections that relate to Washington's political institutions. The last two appointments have been moderate liberals, as befits a capital city with a Democratic president and a Republican Senate. Divided control pressures towards moderation. Whether an appointee is moderately liberal or moderately conservative depends upon the political persuasion of the occupant of the White House.

The American example, then, presents us with difficulties. From one perspective, 'we, the People' vicariously select our Justices through the electoral process and must live with the consequences. There is a problem with lags when the political balance alters; Justices serve until they choose to retire or the grim reaper anticipates them. So there is usually a number of Justices who still reflect a bygone age. But patience will normally witness a change. However, the majority in Washington is never the same as the majority in each of the separate states of the Union. It often happens that the laws and regulations of individual states are struck down by the Court in Washington. Indeed, there are many more examples of this form of activism than there are examples of the court striking down federal laws. Whenever this occurs, there will surely be voices raised in protest and those voices will quickly shift their ground from a selfish disappointment that their side lost, to a principled attack on the majority of the Court who have had the temerity to impose their judgement of constitutionality or legality over those of the people's representatives. As I shall suggest in the next chapter, such a knee-jerk reaction is evidence of a very simple view of democracy indeed.

Conservatism and the Social Origin of Judges

Judges, let us make no mistake about it, are very different from the average man or woman on the Clapham omnibus. So, too, are bishops. Their backgrounds are normally middle class, bookish, often affluent. As Dr Benjamin Spock observed, 'most middle-class whites have no idea what it feels like to be subjected to police who are routinely suspicious, rude, belligerent, and brutal'. Lest it be thought that such a view has a place only in the United States and only at a particular period of time, it is salutary to be reminded that racial discrimination has recently been shown to be prevalent in parts of the British police forces. It is not difficult to make the case, then, that judges can hardly appreciate the conditions of those upon whom they are supposed to judge.

There is a curious paradox here. There is the argument that I have just set out that judges are deemed to be enemies of the people and tend, in many cases, to act against the wishes of the common man, because their views are more *liberal* than the general population would like. Yet, this Spockian argument presumes that, if judges were closer to the people in their upbringings, they would be more sympathetic and less *conservative* in their judgements. Let me leave this little paradox aside for the moment and merely note again that there may well be no necessary connection between social distance and conservatism after all.

There are many different ways in the world by which men and women become judges. Take, for illustration, the fifty states of the United States of America. Twelve states employ partisan elections in which candidates run under the label of their political party. A further twelve states have non-partisan elections in which candidates compete, but without any party identification being explicit. Eight states follow the federal model, with the governor nominating the judges. Four states leave the selection to the legislature, while the remaining fourteen employ what is called a merit plan. Under this scheme a judicial nominating board of judges, lawyers and lay persons is established to scrutinize applications, after which it sends a shortlist of the most suitable candidates to the governor for final selection. Most judges hold office for fixed terms, which can normally be renewed. In some states there is provision for recall, so that judges can be voted off the state's highest court. This happened recently in California, where three judges, including the Chief Justice Rose Bird, were recalled, basically because it was thought by many articulate Californians that they held too-liberal views and were not prepared to impose the death penalty.

In France, there is a corps of professional civil servants whose complete career is bound up with the courts, either as prosecutor or as judge (and for a few individuals both, at different times during their active lives). Access to the profession is gained automatically after graduation from the National School for the Magistracy, to which about 250 students are admitted each year from over 1,000 hopefuls. Young graduates start their careers on the lower rungs of the judicial hierarchy, minor magistrates or judges of small and not very important courts and, if all goes well, they get promoted regularly until they reach the pinnacle of the ordinary court system, the *Cour de Cassation*. The treatment of members of this corps is akin to most other civil service institutions and advancement is derived in part from sheer ability, part from being in the right place at the right time, and part from appearing a safe pair of hands to superiors with the authority for promotions. The *Conseil Constitutionel* is the exception. For this court, the appointment process is highly political. Its nine members, whose term of office is limited, are in the gift of the President of the Republic, the President of the Senate and the Presiding Officer in the National Assembly. Their choices are rarely the career judges; more often they are academics or, most common of all, senior or retired politicians.

It is rare indeed for a Justice of the United States Supreme Court not to have had some political experience. There, too, the process is highly political. Presidents always keep an eye on what kind of judicial philosophy will best help their political programme and seek out men and women who are likely to hold that philosophy. However, the process also involves the Senate, which must confirm all nominations before they can become Justices, and Senators have their agendas too. About one quarter of all nominees have failed to be confirmed. Presidents are also mindful of other political needs and will use their nominations to advance secondary strategies as well. When a vacancy occurred in 1986, the front-running ideological candidate was Robert Bork, but close behind him came Antonin Scalia.

That Bork lost out was due in part to his age and his smoking (Scalia seemed likely to remain on the Court longer) and partly because Reagan fancied he would gain a little political advantage by nominating the first ever Italian-American to the Court. A somewhat similar calculation had been present when he had made his first nomination. He had promised on the campaign trail that one of his first nominees would be a woman. When Potter Stewart surprised most observers by retiring, the pressure on Reagan to make his first nomination a woman was extreme and Sandra Day O'Connor was the most qualified conservative female jurist he could find. But his ideological, and programmatic, goals would have been better served by somebody else.

Whatever the actual procedures, there is abundant and unsurprising evidence that the people who reach the courts of last resort are men and women from educated, middle-class backgrounds, some of the ablest people of their generation, almost certainly educated in the more elite universities and institutes. They may originally have come from humble beginnings, but for virtually all of their adult life, they would have been in the fast stream, well paid, well regarded, self-confident, and increasingly divorced from the experiences of the poorest and least competent members of society. Judges are part of every country's elite; they are very frequently scions of that elite. Certainly, they share many of the patterns of thought and behaviour of the elite.

For some observers of the British scene, this very fact ensures a high bench that is almost certainly to be conservative and woefully out of touch with ordinary people's concerns. This, at any rate, was John Griffiths's position in the late 1970s. And it is simple to see why he should have thought that. The British pathway to the highest positions in the judiciary can indeed be described in a way that leads to a presumption of conservative bias. To be minimally qualified, a potential judge must be a barrister, preferably a Queen's Counsel (QC). To become a barrister requires, in the initial years after qualification, when the briefs are few and the income small, a private income to tide over the lean years. This partial self-selection is then accentuated by the internal reviews through which promotion, first to QC and then to the bench, take place. The performance as barrister and, later, as judge is noted by senior figures in the profession and the final choice of the Lord Chancellor depends upon those estimations, in which a single negative observation may well mean exclusion from the charmed circle of high flyers. Thus, in Griffiths's words, the senior judges 'have by their education and training and the pursuit of their profession as barristers, acquired a strikingly homogeneous collection of attitudes, beliefs and principles, which to them represent the public interest'. This vision tended to be out of sympathy with trade unionist positions and Labour party policies.

While this exaggerates the position that John Griffiths put forward in his *The Politics of the Judiciary*, it reflects a view that has been widely held by people on the left. That view has been reinforced by enough decisions to make it appear not only a description of reality but an explanation for conservative outcomes. The great decisions of the 1970s, when Labour was in office, seemed to represent the triumph of the Tories through judicial means when the ballot box had driven them from office. The 'fares fair' case, which I described in the first chapter was one, the decision overruling the Labour government's attempt to impose comprehensive education on the Tameside local authority was another; and the actions of the National Industrial Relations Court were inevitably seen as a further illustration.

Such a view is not new. The outcry in 1909 over the Taff Vale case, when a union was for the first time held to be responsible for the financial loss caused by a strike, was a powerful force behind the political rise of Labour and the Liberal Government's

Trade Union legislation. In 1911, Winston Churchill (not normally known as a figure ready to pillory the Establishment) suggested to the House of Commons that 'where class issues are involved...it is impossible to pretend that the courts command the same degree of general confidence. On the contrary, they do not, and a very large number of our population have been led to the opinion that they are, unconsciously no doubt, biased'. Some would have been less charitable and felt the bias was conscious.

This is a caricature of reality, although it has a basis in reality. By the 1990s, the exclusion of solicitors from the ranks of lawyers eligible for preferment to a judgeship had been eliminated, except for the Courts of Appeal and the Judicial Committee. The normal procedures had not changed much. In the Lord Chancellor's department information is kept on potential judges (for barristers on pink cards, for solicitors on yellow ones) and contains a range of appreciations and comments, some related to earlier stages in a person's career – on becoming a QC or recorder, for example – and others on performances as barrister or as recorder. Reputations can be made and spread through the cosy world of senior lawyers, just as reputations can be tarnished.

In principle, the choice of preferment, very much a patronage appointment, is meritocratic and Lord Chancellors naturally always stress this point, but the evaluation of some judges and some chairmen of local bar associations surely carry special weight. The secrecy of the proceedings means that we cannot be sure, but there is little doubt that Sir John Donaldson, because he had been President of the Conservative-created National Industrial Regulations Court, was unpopular with Labour politicians and had to wait for the Labour government to fall before being elevated in 1979 to become a Lord Justice of Appeal and in 1982 Master of the Rolls. By the late 1990s, the reports, while still forming a major part of the evidence upon which a Lord Chancellor would make his recommendations, were less decisive and it became possible for individuals to put themselves forward, virtually to apply, for the job. But the most senior judges do indeed look a very elitist group. Since the brightest Englishmen of their generation in the 1940s and 1950s *did* for the most part go to Oxford or Cambridge Universities for some of their education, it is hardly surprising that the highest benches are now full of Oxbridge graduates. If we look at the Judicial Committee of the House of Lords in 1996 and also the four other major figures in the judicial system (the Lord Chancellor, the Lord Chief Justice, with responsibility for the criminal side of the appeal process, the Master of the Rolls, with responsibility for the civil side, and the Vice-Chancellor) prior to the changes enforced on the government by Lord Taylor's resignation on grounds of ill health, we still find a social profile that is unrepresentative of lawyers generally and the general populace in particular. However, it is a profile that is not entirely devoid of wider experiences and possibly different perspectives.

Every one of the fifteen judges, except for Lord Woolf, studied at either Oxford or Cambridge. Among those who went to British schools, only the Lord Chief Justice, who was educated at Newcastle Grammar School, did not go to an independent school. This almost perfect fit of 'public school and Oxbridge' breaks down very slightly when consideration is taken of the universities where these men (there are no women) obtained their first degrees. Lords Keith and Mackay studied at Edinburgh University, Lord Jauncey at Glasgow University, Lord Slynn at Goldsmith's College, Lord Nicholls at Liverpool University, while no less than three of this group originate from South Africa, Lord Steyn taking his first degree at Stellenbosch University, while both Lord Hoffman and Sir Richard Scott are graduates of the University of Cape Town. While the latter three are indeed Oxbridge graduates, they certainly do not share the same kind of Establishment conformity as used to be the case.

The problem with arguing from social origins to judicial bias are at least twofold. In the first place, the evidence of the last fifteen years shows that the judges have been as prepared to use their judicial power against Conservative governments as against Labour governments, and so there is no simple partisan match between the procedures for reaching the pinnacles of the judicial system and the parties likely to be supported. In the second place, there is a logical difficulty. The argument can all too easily follow this path: if courts were politically conservative, they would come down against trade unions; they do come down against trade unions, therefore they are politically conservative. But there may be very good jurisprudential rules that would have reached the same conclusion, regardless of the judges' predilections. The single jurimetric study of the Law Lords, although based inevitably on a relatively small number of cases, showed interestingly that judges appointed by Labour governments did not vote in any significantly different way from those appointed by Conservative governments. While an obvious partisanship is difficult to show (and is rare among judges, as chapter two indicated), there is nevertheless a real balance towards conserving the *status quo* and thus being conservative with a small 'c'.

Consider for a moment two recent observations about the British judiciary. On the fight against crime, one government official told a journalist from *The Times*, 'the judges are seen as the last bastion of the liberal establishment'. At virtually the same time, the *Economist* referred to 'most senior judges as true arch-conservatives'. How can there be such a paradox? The former, as befits active politicians, is concerned with substance and outcomes; the latter, as a commentator on the legal system as a whole, is more concerned with process. Focusing on process does fit with a broader conception that judges are a conservative force. There are several paths to this conclusion. One concentrates on the legal method and the conventions under which judges perform their job. The argument that the law should be known and consistent automatically pressurizes judges towards continuing the *status quo*. The importance of *stare decisis*, the principle that judges should stand by past decisions, results in a conscious reaffirmation of existing interpretations rather than a readiness to take seriously arguments for change. It was better that bad law should survive so that citizen and legal adviser alike knew where they stood rather than that the law should continuously evolve to fit with changing values and aspirations. Hence, the very conception of law as providing certainties in an uncertain world and as operating predictably in various situations had a powerful hold over practitioners and hence a conserving – a truly conservative – consequence.

The commitment to *stare decisis* was, until 1966, the most central principle of judging in the appeal courts. But it was not always seen as so virtuous. Viscount Philip Snowden once observed: 'To quote me the authority of *precedents* leaves me quite unmoved. All human progress has been made by ignoring precedents. If mankind had continued to be the slave of precedent, we should still be living in caves and subsisting on shellfish and wild berries'. Here is the very crux of the problem. For most scholars of the law, its purpose is not to help progress or to instigate moral improvements but to provide a framework of rights and duties by which a citizen can order his or her life. For most judges, most of the time, the same view is held. But the time does come when decisions handed down in the past no longer make good sense and judges feel it appropriate to revisit them and, if necessary, reverse them. The United States Supreme Court has always exercised this power, not often it should be noted, but regularly enough to assist in keeping the Constitution in tune with the felt necessities of the day. In 1966 the Judicial Committee of the House of Lords decided that it would follow suit.

A focus that is directed exclusively on the social sources of judges and on the principles of judging will direct attention quite rightly towards unrepresentativeness and a readiness to uphold the *status quo*. But the focus is incomplete and the conclusions to be drawn not immediately the obvious ones. Legal training, as with most things, changes over time and grows in line with developments elsewhere in a nation's culture. The liberal Justices of the 1960s in the United States were in part the product of their political nominators (but remember that Earl Warren, William Brennan and Potter Stewart were nominated by the Republican Dwight Eisenhower), but they also reflected, as did the law clerks with whom they worked, a fresh approach to the law. Similarly, the judges in the United Kingdom in the 1980s and 1990s also were part of a jurisprudential shift in the legal community as a whole. They had read their Dworkin. His *Taking Rights Seriously**, while not immune to criticism, certainly established a credible case for seeing judging as a principled activity that would inevitably lead to a certain creativity on the part of the judge. This was consonant with an increasingly rights-based culture thrust forward by the events of 1968. In short, individuals can develop their comprehension intellectually rather than remain merely a product of early upbringing, and this growth is reflective of changing values or, we might say, changing expressions of popular, even democratic, preferences.

Influences on judges are varied in kind and variable in intensity and this is reflected in the disagreements between judges,

*Ronald Dworkin, *Taking Rights Seriously: new impressions with a reply to critics*, Duckworth, London: 1978.

wherever we look, showing that there is little uniformity in responses to the novel and difficult cases coming before them. Having said that, it remains true that the dominant value of all judges in states priding themselves on the rule of law is that the law should be known and consistent and that, *ceteris paribus,* the decisions of those empowered explicitly by the political system authoritatively to allocate values should be upheld. They normally are. What is most striking about courts, even when they come under attack for their activism (which means no more than striking down public laws or regulations or the exercise of discretionary power), is the extent to which they legitimize governments by upholding their actions.

Power and Legitimacy

If the discourse that dominates is a language couched in terms of judges against the people, its protagonists will, in the contemporary age, prevail. With the nearly universal positive connotations given to the need to reflect popular preferences rather than elite priorities, dominating the discourse in this way, or shifting the language to other concepts, is a major point of competition between the sides. Yet it should not necessarily be so. The distinguished American judge Frank Coffin argues that 'when rhetoric is put aside, the judiciary is, in its own matrix of mechanisms, at least as accountable as its sister branches', but he would say that, wouldn't he? Yet his view embraces two important perceptions. First, that judges are more accountable than is often made out and, second, that the most obvious political institutions are less accountable than is usually imagined. Both are worthy of brief examination.

Accountability is a slippery concept. It can mean two quite distinct things. In the first place, it can refer to a relationship in which a person who exercises power over others can be called to account directly for that exercise of power. Elections are the most common way by which such accountability is enforced and the democratic principle depends upon the rulers being endorsed or denied at regular intervals through the ballot box. In some countries, this relationship applies to judges as it does to a whole raft of officials who are empowered to exercise authority over the citizenry. In the United States, for example, it is of course common to elect mayors and sheriffs, school boards and transport managers, but lesser posts, such as the drain commissioner in Cleveland, are also elected. In some states, the recognition of the power inherent in the judiciary is reflected in the establishment of an electoral connection between judge and voter. Such direct linkage between the judiciary and the citizenry is the exception, because most systems pay at least lip service to the idea that the judicial function is qualitatively different from the political function and that it is not the kind of function for which elections are appropriate. The principle of the separation of powers has always been seen as an essential part of any constitutional system designed to control the tendency for rulers to aggregate more and more powers and behave increasingly without regard to the ruled. Power does *tend* to corrupt, as Lord Acton famously said, and absolute power corrupts absolutely. Too many years in office, whether we are looking at the African continent or within Europe to Italy and the United Kingdom, does seem to foster among the governing group an overly developed sense of righteousness.

Nor should we be altogether persuaded that elections do, in fact, result in governments that reflect the wishes and priorities of the governed. Electoral systems, whether the single member plurality system (which exaggerates the margin of victory and underrepresents small parties) or some variant of proportional representation (which exaggerates the significance of the middle ground, around which any viable coalition will be built) all contain some bias. Additionally, while parties offer a collage of policies from which the electorate can chose, the particular combination that is 'bought' rarely, if ever, accurately reflects the actual combination of policies a majority of the citizens would prefer. Normally, there are policies in several parties' offerings that are attractive, but the choices on offer are not sufficiently sophisticated and well calibrated to map on to the electorate's real preferences. So, a simple dichotomy between elected politicians as the bearers of the People's wishes and unelected judges as the bearers of personal preferences needs to be taken with a very large pinch of salt indeed.

But accountability has two further meanings. Officials may be said to be accountable when they make an account of, explain and defend, their actions in the public view. This is most regularly seen in the investigative and oversight committees in the United States Congress, the select committees in the House of Commons or their equivalents in continental Europe. There is no direct link between this form of accountability and retention of office, but it is normally the case that an inadequate defence or a policy roundly condemned will result in some form of retribution, if not immediately, then soon afterwards. Judges are not called to account in this way, but they do explain with considerable precision why they have reached the decisions that they have.

Unlike politicians, whose votes tell the outside world nothing except that votes have been cast in a particular way, judicial opinions set out the logic through which a conclusion has been reached, the evidence on which that decision was based, and the extent to which it conforms or departs from existing precedents.

It is a very public form of explanation, open to consideration and dispute, undeniable and permanent. Judges open their explanations to full view and may expect an open riposte if their logic is thought to be faulty or their balance of interests incorrect. Much of the feedback comes from the academic community and some judges are more aware of this than others. The Justices of the United States Supreme Court enjoy the help of three or four law clerks, very bright graduates from the best law schools who act as assistants to a Justice for a single year, and they bring to the Justices' attention the new ideas and approaches of the current professoriate, the academic criticisms of the Justice's work, and the perspective of another generation. The senior judges in the United Kingdom lack this kind of regular access to the responsive world, although some do make an effort to keep abreast of current thinking. So, judges in most countries are extremely accountable in the sense of making a clear account of their actions.

There is, too, a third sense of accountability, one that is less direct than the electoral connection and less open than the publication of opinions. This is the sense in which officials take account of the likely responses of affected groups and individuals, anticipate their reactions, and adjust their actions to match what is possible and practicable. The degree to which this form of accountability is utilized depends very much on the autonomous powers available to the official. A commanding officer in the military need give little attention to it and a politician without the potential constraints of elections similarly need give little attention to it in the short run. But judges are different.

In earlier chapters, I have stressed the power of the courts, emphasized the way in which many of the decisions that they take have political ramifications and are legislative in effect, and built up the judicial branch into a major player in the game of politics. That is why concern is expressed about their behaviour. But the judiciary has virtually no autonomous power. It is, as Alexander Hamilton observed when trying to persuade the voters of New York state to ratify the United States Constitution, 'the least dangerous branch of government, because it enjoys the power of neither the purse nor the sword'. Quite unlike the government of a country that can reward or penalize the subjects by tax or welfare policies and that can enforce its writ, as those who protest against the building of motorways know, through the use of police, bailiffs and even soldiers, courts produce merely a piece of paper and expect that its judgements will be upheld. They usually are. It is interesting that Michael Howard appealed against very few of his 'defeats' and it is educative to consider why this might be.

The effectiveness of courts comes to the heart of a legitimate political system. People obey instructions for a variety of reasons: fear of retribution, fear of public humiliation, apathy, convention, personal support for a policy, an internalized sense of obligation to do so. The greater the sense of legitimacy – this internalized sense of obligation that represents a genuine acceptance that a particular public authority has a *right* to give instructions and have them obeyed – the smoother a society functions and the more effective are its institutions. Courts depend hugely on this legitimacy. So long as they march side-by-side with the executive, as they do in socialist countries with little or no attachment to the idea of the separation of powers, they know that the coercive powers of the state will be on their side. But once they act against the wishes and interests of the other branches, they depend only upon their moral authority and the respect in which they are held. Justice Sandra Day O'Connor wrote in 1987: 'The Court cannot buy support for its decisions by spending money and, except to a minor degree, it cannot independently coerce obedience to its decrees. The Court's power lies, rather, in its legitimacy, a product of substance and perception that shows itself in people's acceptance of the Judiciary as fit to determine what the Nation's law means and to declare what it demands'.

This, finally, says something important about democracy, which I will elaborate in the next chapter. Democracy is, of course, intimately related to the procedures by which the governed choose their governors and hold them to account. Democracy without some form of elections, some form of popular mandate, could hardly be a democracy at all. But democracy is a great deal more than that. It embraces the conditions in which free citizens can make intelligent choices, rules that set limits to what governors can do and establishes rights that the governed can expect to be honoured, and the means by which these adjuncts to crude expressions of majority rule may be realised. The means are laws and constitutions, on the one hand, with the judges who monitor and apply them, on the other. When the judges are accused of going against the People by countermanding the actions taken by politicians in their name (but not always with their knowledge or their full support), they are often protecting democratic forms that are, in the longer run, the People's own protection against tyranny.

4

JUDGES AS HEROES

The ideas that judges may frequently be acting against the People and be a force for conservatism derives largely from a very romantic notion of the People. These charges tend to originate from politicians who see themselves as the repository of the People's wishes and priorities as a result of their electoral successes, or from commentators of the Left who impose on the People the progressive views that they themselves hold and that, they are sure, would be held more widely if many of the forces at work in the world – the media, the educational system, the social structure – had been less biased. There are strengths in both these positions. But there are fundamental weaknesses and, sometimes, contradictions in them as well. The empirical evidence, for one thing, indicates that the highest courts more often lend their seal of approval to the politicians' actions than otherwise and, in so doing, strengthen the legitimacy of the government. Of course, this may well be to uphold conservative laws and ignore the claims of disadvantaged citizens against the powerful state, but there is no automatic connection between the use of judicial power and the discomfort of liberal governments. Far from it; both Mr Howard and President Reagan would offer evidence that the senior judges in their countries had been too liberal.

In this chapter, I want to go further than argue merely that some of the criticisms of the judges are misplaced (some are well made, and I do not want to dispute that). This defence of judges makes two quite different points, each of which deserves careful analysis.

The first is a normative argument that political systems need judiciaries to restrain the undemocratic and unacceptable actions of those in power. The second, which has no necessary logical connection with the first, claims that judges are especially well qualified to take on the role of guardians. Let us take them in turn.

There is, of course, a vast and enduring literature on the ideal political system and on the true nature of democracy. It reflects our inability to develop a system of resolving society's competing needs and wants that gathers broad acceptance and support. When Francis Fukuyama claimed to have discovered the 'End of History', he was essentially arguing that the socialist experiment had failed and the liberal alternative had won the war of ideas. The problem with such triumphalism is that it simplifies out of existence the very real difficulties inherent in the liberal alternative and ignores the reality that other models, most obviously those arising from an Islamic world view, are very much in existence and competing for support. This last, but extremely important, point I will not follow up here, but the difficulties with the liberal alternative need a little attention.

Democratic has become the praise word for political systems in the 1990s. The former socialist bloc countries seek the accolade; multilateral organizations such as the World Bank or the International Monetary Fund increasingly see it as a condition for assistance, and the industrialized nations pride themselves upon it. Yet democracy is a slippery concept, hard to pin down and relatively easy to claim. Two strands are worth emphasizing at the outset, because they speak directly to the role of judges in a modern political system.

The first strand is what may be called the classic American

model. This involves four important presumptions. First, government, although necessary, is potentially dangerous because it is the only institution that can claim the legitimate use of the state's power to enforce policies upon the governed. Second, arising from the first proposition, people must have a direct control over who exercises state power and the opportunity regularly to call its governors to account. At the same time, the limitations on that power, themselves necessary because of the potential inherent in state power and even the people's tendency to get carried away emotionally, need to be clearly spelled out and applied. Finally, if the people are to perform their obligations properly, it is essential that there should be full and free discussion of all alternatives. This view recognizes that, ultimately, power must depend on the consent of the governed but, equally as important, that the governed themselves cannot be guaranteed to ensure good government. Such a view rests upon a realistic appraisal of the weaknesses of men and women. In James Madison's wonderfully simple words, 'if men were angels, there would be no need of government'. These presumptions need complex constitutional forms if they are to be realised.

The second strand begins less with the need for controls on government (itself a partial vote of no confidence in the people's ability to order society successfully) and more with the rights of the people. It recognizes that, in the large states of the present epoch, there must be intermediaries between the people and those who govern, although the spread of electronic means of communication may make possible, but perhaps not desirable, the establishment of 'Friday night is political choice night', when the electors code in their special numbers and vote directly on the issues of the day. Any form of representation is a derogation from an individual's sovereignty. Those to whom the important task of governing is entrusted must create an agenda, argue for it, obtain electoral support for it and attempt to put it into practice. It sounds simple enough, but the details of that agenda are where the trouble begins. It might well not map on to the distribution of views held across a country. Its one major theme may win it support despite a host of smaller unwanted accoutrements. It might endorse treatment of some citizens that, while popular, diminishes their rights. So we return to two of the themes that have been around and about us throughout the book, but rarely centre stage: those who claim democratic power may have won elections, but that does not automatically mean that they reflect accurately the People's will. The emphasis on electoral sources of power leaves too much aside the question of whether there may be rights that no electoral majority should be permitted to abridge. The role of the courts has, in some countries, been to ensure that these last glosses on the liberal experiment are protected against the popular passions of the passing moment.

Changing Views of the Judges' Role

The country in which to begin such a review is the United States. At one stage in its history, this would have seemed a curious enterprise. For the first 150 years after the ratification of the Constitution, the Supreme Court appeared to play the role of protecting the strong against the weak, when it was not legitimising the national government's expansive power claims. It maintained that Dred Scott, once a slave, was always a slave even when resident in a 'free' state. It emasculated the equal protection clause of the Fourteenth Amendment by sanctioning 'separate but equal' facilities for whites and blacks (and it came to take a somewhat uncritical view of what constituted equal) and severely limited the reach of the Civil Rights Acts passed immediately after the Civil War. It favoured the sanctity of contracts, even if that meant long and dangerous working hours and it sided with companies and corporations when the regulatory state interfered with their freedoms. While there were occasions when this general bias slipped and the regulation of the strong in the presumed interests of the many was permitted, the overall impression is one that epitomizes the Court as the protector of the strong rather than as a defence for the weak. Certainly, the Bill of Rights, those ten Amendments added to the Constitution in the first Congress as a promise for ratification, had not prevented the governments of the several states restricting the rights of unfavoured minorities and individuals.

As always, the story is muddied by decisions that appear on their face to be inconsistent. What is at least incontrovertible is that the exercise of judicial power was recognized as legitimate and was employed on occasions against governments, both national and state. The excessively democratic underpinnings of jurisprudence in countries such as the Soviet Union and the People's Republic of China, although they had their populist supporters, were almost entirely absent. In those socialist regimes, the starting assumptions have been that the government must, because of its class nature, represent the public interest and the democratic mandate and, second, that party decisions enjoy a higher status, because of their immediacy to the People, than any other. Courts, therefore, act in a democratic fashion if, and only if, they support the positions taken by those who claim to represent the public interest, that is the party leadership and the governmental structures through which they operate. Hence, judges legitimate and support whatever the political branches sanction.

Populist philosophies in the United States may sometimes start down that route, arguing that the people's representatives express the public interest through legislation and that courts have no business double-guessing the considered priorities and preferences of those who speak on behalf of the sovereign people. But populists, while wedded to the decisions of governments close to themselves, are always nervous of distant governments and seek ways to inhibit them. In this picture, local judges may well be elected and representative of the popular view and so ensure that the democratic wish is fulfilled (and juries most certainly should play an important role). Yet judges will also be needed to check the excessive powers of higher governmental organs and keep them within the limited bounds consciously set by the Constitution itself. In other words, local laws and the actions of local officials should be deemed legal and proper and adjudicated within the confines of the local political order, but national laws and the actions of national officials need to be considered by a Supreme Court, ready to use judicial power to restrain them.

The difficulty with such a view is not only that each level of government may regulate the same area of human activity (such as transport, where much policy must cross state boundaries) but that the Fourteenth Amendment appears to set down national limitations upon states; they may not deny to any person within their jurisdiction the equal protection of the laws or due process of law. Now, it is by no means obvious what these phrases mean or clear as to what matters they might cover. Some progressive states used their powers to regulate businesses, setting limitations on the number of hours employees might be required to work and promulgating regulations that asserted minimum wage laws. Some businesses saw this as an infringement of their rights to liberty and property. At the beginning of the century, the Supreme Court upheld one set of claims arguing that minimum hours laws constrained the possibility of, say, bakers to contract to work for their employers more than 60 hours in a week if they so wished. On the other hand, they upheld limitations on women's hours of work in order to protect what the Justices considered to be the weaker sex from arrangements that were thought to be against their health interests.

For the most part, however, the Supreme Court accepted the constitutionality of state laws so long as they were rationally related to a legitimate function of government or, to put it more crudely, so long as there was some conceivable (if strained) justification for the law and the state was entitled to regulate in that area. Few laws were thus struck down and few individuals could look to the courts for redress against state action. So the Supreme Court accepted segregatory practices in the southern states, laws that discriminated against women, qualifications that effectively disenfranchised many citizens, and police practices that limited suspect rights. It was the already powerful, majorities in state legislatures and business corporations, who far more often than not prevailed in litigation. Observers in, say, 1936 would not have thought it worth much time to argue about the courts being bastions of minority rights. Generally speaking, they were not.

The last fifty years would paint the Court in a very different light. The litany of liberal decisions since the end of the Second World War is striking indeed: *Shelley v. Kraemer* outlawed restricted covenants; *Brown v. Board of Education* (perhaps the best known of all Supreme Court cases) outlawed racial discrimination in elementary education: *Miranda v. Arizona* established procedural safeguards for suspects; *Gideon v. Wainwright* asserted a constitutional right to a lawyer; *Reynolds v. Sims* required the population of each electoral district to be equal and thus constitutionally established the principle of one man, one vote, one value; *Swann v. Charlotte-Mecklenburg* permitted compulsory bussing as a method of integrating schools; *Frontiero v. Richardson* outlawed most discrimination on grounds of gender;

Regents of the University of California v. Bakke gave constitutional blessing to affirmative action on grounds of race; *Johnson v. Santa Clara County* did the same thing for gender; *Roe v. Wade* (perhaps the second best known of decisions) established a woman's right to an abortion. And so I could go on.

This dramatic change did not take place without considerable disagreement among the Justices themselves nor without powerful objections from the wider political community. To explain it, we need two quite distinct types of argument. The first is a technical one, setting out how the judicial philosophy of a majority of the Court altered and how this new philosophy became broadly accepted. In the 1920s, the Court had decided that no state could reasonably claim to practice 'due process' if the freedom of speech and of the press was inhibited. By the late 1930s, a majority of the Court felt that the phrase 'due process' should cover the absolutely essential prerequisites for a civilized society and argued that some of the protections against the national government built into the first ten Amendments to the Constitution (the Bill of Rights) should be applied against the states as well. In the subsequent quarter of a century, the Court came to incorporate into the 'due process' clause virtually all the rights adopted in 1791. This explains how the Court came to defend the rights of free speech and assembly (developed into a right to communication) and the rights of suspects and those on trial.

A second philosophical development led to a more stringent examination of what would count as rational. In 1960, Jennifer Hoyt appealed to the Supreme Court against the death sentence imposed upon her in Florida, arguing that she had been denied the 'equal protection of the laws' and 'due process of law' as a result of the way juries were chosen in the state. All men were required to be on the list of potential jurors; women, however, could choose to be included, but were not required to be. The legislators argued that, since a woman's primary duty was to look after the home, family and children, it would be inappropriate to make jury service a requirement. Mrs Hoyt's murder of her husband followed a long period of abuse and arguments and she felt that her case would have been considered somewhat differently if the jury had not been entirely male. The Supreme Court in 1961 found that Florida's jury regulations were quite rational and upheld her conviction for first degree murder. By 1970, it had changed its mind about the legally differentiated treatment of women and it increasingly struck down state laws that it felt lacked a rational base. When it came to laws and regulations that differentiated on grounds of race, it took a very much stronger line and argued that such differentiation could only meet the requirements of the equal protection clause if the regulation was necessary for the purposes of government and was the only practicable way of achieving that purpose. Virtually no law could meet such stringent criteria and the panoply of racially discriminatory laws was steadily dismantled.

The second line of argument is a political one. It notes that ideas develop, that old conventional wisdoms may give way to new, that a society's public agenda alters over time, and that the composition of the judiciary follows these changes. There is no doubt that attitudes to race after the Second World War did shift, especially among the better educated and more internationalist members of American society, and that conceptions of equality began to move away from an unthinking attachment to equality of opportunity towards a greater concern for equality of outcome. The men whom presidents nominated to the Supreme Court came increasingly from a pool of lawyers who had taken on board the new ideas about the purpose of law and the central role of the Bill of Rights in the constitutional system. What happened in the courts and what happened in Washington were not synchronized, but they moved in the same direction. The Civil Rights Act of 1964 and other parts of Lyndon Johnson's Great Society programme had their echoes in the decisions of the Supreme Court and the commitment, through the Department of Justice, to applying the new laws. The Court's new interpretations of the Constitution was another indication of how the political and judicial branches worked side by side.

In recent years, a tension has gown up between the two branches of government. Part of the Reagan revolution was supposed to include a rolling back of judicial power, a reversal of many of the liberal decisions made by the Court in previous years, and the re-establishment of a Court that deferred much more to elected governments and their officials and much less to individual citizens challenging them. Many conservatives applauded this attempt and campaigned strongly for men like Robert Bork to be elevated to the Supreme Court. Others, however, feared precisely that. To the underprivileged and the poor, the unconventional and the unlucky, the Court had seemed to be the mainstay of their hopes. The Justices were indeed their heroes, rather than the activist villains depicted by people such as Attorney-General Edwin Meese. Which position one espouses depends, in the real world, on which position advances one's interest best, but it ought also to be rooted in a conception of democracy. For those who do not have complete faith in the people's representatives to act fairly and fear the tyranny of the majority, courts with teeth are essential. To those who believe that democracy is little more than another word for majority rule, activist judges are inevitably a source of concern.

In Defence of the Citizen
The very existence of a phrase such as 'redress of grievance' suggests that in the United Kingdom there might well be grievances needing redress. In classical British constitutional theory, the proper avenue for any such concern would be through a minister's responsibility to Parliament for the action of his or her department. The effectiveness of this principle has increasingly been called into question and successive governments have found themselves forced to accept that, as the welfare state and the interventionist tentacles of the state increasingly affected ordinary people's lives, new institutions were required to deal with legitimate complaints about, say, the calculation of a benefit to which somebody may be entitled or the justification of a planning decision with wide local and personal repercussions. In place of the blanket principle of ministerial responsibility has grown up a veritable battery of alternative channels, from the Ombudsman (strictly speaking, the Parliamentary Commissioner for Administration), through statutory tribunals and the establishment of the National Audit Office to a reorganisation, through the 1981 Supreme Court Act, making the judicial review of administrative action more easily available to the ordinary person.

There are many lessons to be learned from this development. Which is emphasized depends upon the observer's particular concern. It is notable, for example, that Parliament as an institution has steadily become less and less effective at calling a minister to order and at protecting individuals from the arbitrary, and perhaps illegal, acts of those working on the state's behalf. One could emphasize the very different context of the relationship between citizen and state when contrasted with fifty years ago. On the one hand, the administrative state has obviously permeated an extraordinarily extensive range of human activities and has become a very central influence on everyday life. On the other hand, the individual citizen has increasingly felt that the power of the state needs closer oversight and has been ready to seek that. So far as this book is concerned, perhaps the most critical point is to draw attention to the way in which the courts have been drawn into arguments between state and subject.

Chapter two observed how even governments themselves have, in recent years, pushed the courts out of the wings and more and more on to the political stage as important players in the political game. Here, there is, one might say, less of a self-seeking pull and more of an externally induced push factor. As the existing arrangements for safeguarding individuals against the state became less and less effective, individuals themselves, aided and abetted by the judges on one side and sometimes interest groups on the other, looked to new ways of protecting themselves. New is not really the right word. Judicial review has a long history, but its availability as a means for defending individuals against the state was not widely permitted. The judges had tended to accept the myth of ministerial responsibility and therefore left such claims to Parliament to deal with. The classic expression of this is perhaps *Liversidge v. Anderson*, decided in 1942. Here, a minister had detained Liversidge on the grounds that he had information that convinced him that the detained man would have been a danger to the state. However, he refused to present the evidence for rebuttal. A majority of the Law Lords found in favour of the minister, giving considerable weight to the 'facts' that he was a person of credibility and responsible to Parliament. Lord Macmillan summarized this view when observing that the emergency powers had been conferred upon 'one of the high officers of State who, by reason of his position, is entitled to public confidence in his capacity and integrity; who is answerable to Parliament for his conduct in office'.

That decision was handed down slightly more than fifty years ago and at a time of war, when patriotic support for governments is high, but the need for the protection of individual rights is also enhanced. (It is interesting to note that in the United States at the same time, a clear majority of the Supreme Court – including such liberal activists as Hugo Black – permitted the policy of gathering all those of Japanese extraction into camps, whether there was any evidence of hostile action or not). In the subsequent fifty years, the strength of both prongs of Lord Macmillan's argument have been reduced. The judges no longer presume that ministerial responsibility is man enough for the job of protecting individual interests, nor do they treat ministers with the same deference as their predecessors did.

The growth of judicial review in the last few years will be seen as one of the major developments in a constitutional system that, although it prides itself on stability and continuity, has actually undergone dramatic changes. In 1974, there were 160 applications for judicial review; in 1994 there were 3,208. That is a huge percentage rise, but the numbers themselves are not large and appear very modest when one considers that just over 6,000 applications for *certiorari* are made each year to the United States Supreme Court (the Court must grant *certiorari* before it hears it) and that most of the British cases are concerned exclusively with questions of immigration rights. Of those three thousand plus applications, the High Court heard 39 per cent (or 1471) and found against the government on 441 occasions, most of which never made a headline and few of which were appealed. Interpreting these figures, as is so often the case, depends very much upon the vantage point chosen. Considering the thousands and thousands of decisions that are taken in the government's name, this is a very small number of errors indeed. Seen from other end of the telescope, it was accepted that 441 individuals had good reason to believe that their treatment had been illegal or contrary to natural justice or procedurally incorrect, and that is a lot of people if lined up end to end.

There is no Bill of Rights to protect individual rights and freedoms in the United Kingdom and Parliament, in effect the legislating agency for the majority party's leadership, can – and does – quite legally take away what in other countries would be entrenched rights. That is its prerogative. But there has unquestionably been a rising concern that some form of protection of rights ought to be considered seriously. This might merely be the incorporation of the European Convention into British law or it might be the drafting of a quite new document. Exactly to what degree such changes would impinge on the sovereignty of parliament is also a subject of debate. The point of interest in my view is that, across much of the thinking political spectrum, there is a genuine feeling that the British constitutional system can no longer deliver what its citizens want and need, especially in the way of civil and political rights. This is part of a general malaise affecting the political system widely, but it is also reflective of a particular set of concerns. While few would embrace judicial activism with enthusiasm, the logic of much current thought is leading to a position where the judges will have to be the defenders of litigants, normally the least powerful, who challenge the power of the state. This is, indeed, the stuff of which heroes are made.

An Independent Judiciary
It is not only in the United States and the United Kingdom that judges have exercised the judicial power to restrain the actions of

governments and those who work for them. The late twentieth century has come to place less confidence and less faith in governments. Two apparently paradoxical forces have been at work. On the one side, the liberal (indeed, socialist inspired) view of the state as an institution through which communal benefits can be achieved has led to an expanded vision of what governments ought to do. Despite much talk of rolling back the state, citizens still expect governments to resolve problems and, through their public policies, improve the conditions of life. Even conservatives who speak of too much government find themselves, for the most part, obliged to recognize that governments are expected to come to the rescue of farmers who have fallen on hard times or communities who have suffered under the hand of nature. But, in a somewhat contradictory fashion, citizens have increasing doubts as to whether governments will actually act fairly and properly. The deference to politicians is very much reduced. Indeed, surveys have shown an alarmingly low estimation for people given such enormous responsibilities. In a poll at the beginning of 1996, it was found in Britain that politicians ranked even lower in the hierarchy of people's estimation than journalists and estate agents. So there is a demand for action, but a suspicion about those entrusted with that action.

It is little surprise, then, that there has been a readiness to turn to other figures to provide the moral high ground and the means to balance the demands on government against the presumed quality of the governors. Into this space has come the judges. Part of their attraction remains the idealized picture of the judge as a neutral, wise, and fair arbitrator, who will not be pressurized by partisan allegiances or personal predilections, but will hand out Justice. Overstated though this vignette is, it retains extremely important aspects that colour what actually takes place.

It is clear that the image of the non-political judge is a myth. However, it should also be clear that this does not at the same time mean that there is no substance to that myth. Indeed, it would be quite wrong to dispose entirely of it, for two important reasons. In the first place, the myth has an essential place in any system of widely accepted dispute resolution. There is no way to escape the need for courts and judges these days and they must enjoy a status and image that permits their actions to be accepted as legitimate and rightly to be obeyed. The source of that legitimacy lies in the belief, whether true or false, that they act neutrally and advance justice. When this belief is challenged or shattered, there are only two responses, either a loss of faith in the system of dispute resolution or the acceptance that the individual error is an example of the frailty of human nature in a system that is essentially sound. Nobody, and no institution, after all, is so perfect that mistakes do not occur. Too many of the latter quickly generate the more serious response. The importance of symbolism in politics is nowadays too often undervalued. In the area of legal disputes, it is more important than ever that those who have the heavy responsibility of arbitration receive, and deserve to receive, respect.

In several countries, this respect is under strain. Part of the pressure comes from high-profile cases where justice has clearly not been done. These may be occasions when people who later appear to be innocent are initially found guilty and sentenced to long periods of imprisonment (but fortunately, except in the United States, not to death). They may be instances when commonsensical notions of what justice requires is passed by for 'reasons of state' or 'in the national interest' or result in what appear to be sentences unrepresentative of the nature of the crime. Part of the pressure comes from the open challenge to the courts mounted by politicians who, naturally enough, feel upset by decisions with which they disapprove and seek political capital out of attacking them. Short-term gain can soon give way to long-term loss, for the system of governing any country depends, in part, on a dispute resolution process in which people have faith.

In the second place, much of what currently occurs in states, particularly the United Kingdom, makes little sense if the partial reality of the myth is not recognized. Judges are seen as peculiarly well qualified to act neutrally. In the United Kingdom, in particular, there is a tradition – and a temptation – to pass to judges the duty to enquire into matters of political contention when others might be thought unlikely to act objectively. There is a long tradition of this, and the consequences of some, such as Lord Devlin's into the disturbances in Malawi (formerly Nyasaland), have been profound. In recent years, Lord Scarman covered the Brixton riots of 1981 and Justice Taylor enquired into the collapse of a football stand at Sheffield United's Hillsborough ground and the responsibilities for the deaths incurred. Most recently of all, the Major government has turned to two senior judges to carry out enquiries on subjects that were causes of considerable embarrassment to it. Lord Nolan was given the responsibility for creating, in effect, a moral code for those in public life after there had been widespread criticism of backbenchers' receiving money for asking questions in the House of Commons, of civil servants moving quickly into lucrative jobs closely related to their interests when still in government, and of ministers' relations with businesses likely to employ them on their retirement. Sir Richard Scott enquired into the government's behaviour in the arms for Iran affair; and gathered an enormous amount of evidence about possible improprieties, the misleading of the House of Commons, the use of immunity certificates, and a host of allegations that gave the picture of a government prepared to cut any corner or make any deal to advance its short-term political needs.

The regular use of judges for the purpose of examining disasters, such as the Aberfan landslide in South Wales, or allegations of governmental irregularity, or policy issues that divide a party (such as Lord Diplock's report on the place of ordinary courts in Northern Ireland during the troubles), is an indication that the normal procedures of government are not working. Parliamentary or ministerial enquiries would be the appropriate way of giving focused attention to a specific policy issue. But the confrontational ethos and party loyalties within Parliament make it difficult for such tasks to be carried out and their conclusions accepted as fair and reasonable. Increasingly, then, outsiders must be brought in, but even they have begun to suffer from politicians attacking them for their lack of intimate knowledge, or balance, or procedural fairness. When the media had pressed the issue of public morality on to the political agenda, the government turned to another judge.

In other parts of what was once the British empire, the same instinct is found and judges are seen as uniquely suitable for carrying out delicate investigations whose conclusions might well be embarrassing for politicians. It is, perhaps, a peculiarly British, and imperial, perception that judges can resolve crises because of their particular skills and their moral, non-partisan position. When a scandal broke in Zimbabwe about high officials' profiteering from their position, a commission of enquiry headed by a judge was set up to investigate, and it did name names, destroying the power and status of some major political figures, perhaps even pushing one long-time nationalist to commit suicide. In South Africa, the Goldstone Commission uncovered much of what had been hidden by government in the last years of the apartheid system and did a great deal to convince leading politicians of the African National Congress that justice could be discovered by people of any race.

The reason for imagining that judges have a special skill in such instances is twofold. In the first place, the skill and experience needed to extract detailed information from often unwilling witnesses and the need to balance the arguments and evidence from conflicting parties is one that judges, especially those who reach that position as a result of recognized cross-examination skills as barristers, should have to a special degree. That is a good, instrumental reason. In the second place, however, there is the normative argument that the findings of these commissions of enquiry should be seen as non-political, in the sense that they are non-partisan but neutral, based upon a pursuance of the truth, not political advantage. The findings should then be widely accepted and recognized as the truth. The myth of neutrality is here powerfully exposed.

Not all countries turn to judges on such occasions. The United States, for example (with the exception of the Warren Commission on the assassination of President Kennedy) tends to leave such matters to a range of political bodies, to congressional enquiries or presidential commissions and task forces or, latterly, independent counsel or special prosecutors. These latter are nominated by the judicial branch and tend to be activist lawyers, rather than neutral judges. A good example is to follow the country's response to the 'Irangate scandal'. This was the episode during the Reagan Administration when arms were transhipped to conservative forces in Nicaragua, despite laws against that, by doing a deal with the Iranian government, with whom the United States was not supposed to have close diplomatic links.

The Senate instituted its own hearing, the President set up an executive branch enquiry (the Tower Commission) and a special prosecutor was appointed to see whether illegalities had been committed by members of the Administration. The first two were composed entirely of politicians who felt obliged, and able, to enquire in detail about the particular deals struck by members of the executive branch.

Judges, then, do not have a unique capacity to review mounds of evidence, order it, and prepare recommendations (although the performance of the Tower Commission left a good deal to be desired). Even in Britain, others have been given similar charges, such as Lord Franks or Lord Goodman. But they are well prepared for the task. Since most also believe in the myth of neutrality, their biases – such as they are – derive from the inarticulacy of their premises rather than from partisan commitments. They have often championed the underdog against the powers that be, as Devlin did in Nyasaland, and have forced governments, as Nolan did, to take more seriously than they had, widespread popular disquiet about their behaviour.

Justice Hugo Black, although he was considered during his last years on the Court to be part of the conservative minority, had been at the forefront of expanding the protections for individuals against the federal government that were set out in the first ten Amendments to the United States Constitution to cover state governments as well. He clearly saw in this one of the central functions of the judicial branch. 'Under our constitutional system', he wrote, 'courts stand against any winds that blow as havens of refuge for those who might otherwise suffer because they are helpless, weak, outnumbered, or because they are non-conforming victims of prejudice and public excitement'. Here, then, is a passionate defence of the judge's role as hero. It is also a cry of faith from somebody who saw good government as a system that necessitated care for the individual and required, where appropriate, the interests of a single citizen to be held of greater value than the preferences of a majority. It is also a vision generated very much from the perspective of the least powerful and most disadvantaged.

Other respectable traditions exist. While the French republican commitment to government by Assembly does look somewhat tarnished at the end of the twentieth century, the British tradition of parliamentary sovereignty together with the rule of law continues to have its powerful adherents. The weakness of ministerial responsibility as a means of protecting individual rights alongside parliamentary sovereignty has been touched upon, but commitment to the rule of law must envisage a role for judges. No electoral mandate can put a government above the law. Without the opportunity for citizens to challenge government decisions in the courts, the rule of law would be nothing more than an empty phrase. Politicians would otherwise be the judges of their own cause. This reasserts the importance of a separation of powers.

If powers are to be separate and independent (and the purpose of this separation would be lost if the distinct branches of government were not, to some extent, independent), then the judicial branch must be able to check, and check effectively, those who contravene the law. The United States makes such separation as complete as it can be and the same determination to ensure that judges are not subject to pressure from the overtly political branches is found in, say, France and Germany. The United Kingdom prides itself on the independence of its judges, but that is not quite the same thing as establishing a clear separation of powers. In one obvious case, there is manifestly no such separation. The Lord Chancellor not only sits in the Cabinet as a leading figure of the executive, he also acts as the Speaker of the House of Lords (and can play a proactive role in the legislature), and he may sit on the Judicial Committee of the House of Lords, although nowadays the opportunity for this judging is diminished by the burden of work elsewhere. Such pedantries have never really interested the British. What is more important is the real performance of the senior judges and it is their independence that is thought critical.

It is possible to be independent in many ways. Judges may be independent to the extent that they are not in danger of losing their posts for decisions that displease the other branches; British judges are essentially independent in this sense. Judges may be independent in their lack of personal stake in the cases before them and can, therefore, much more easily act as neutral arbiters when trying to resolve a dispute; British judges are essentially independent in this sense. Judges may be independent to the degree that they follow only their own hierarchy of values and understanding of the law and bow to no external pressures on this score; British judges are essentially independent in this sense, too. But it was precisely this latter independence that worried John Griffiths and others, and that created the impression that justice was defined according to middle-class values, and the interests of the established and powerful was applied to conceptions of the national interest. Judges thought themselves impartial, but the balance of their values led to partial results.

There is no escaping that gloss on the virtue of independence. Judges are used to head enquiries and to sit on appeal courts because they are held to have these traits of independence. Without the first two, the purposes of these institutions would be subverted. Judges in the pocket of the prosecutors or judges prepared to whitewash government ineptitude are well known, but they are not heroes. However, the third sense of independence does cause some concern. If the independence is the independence of the philosopher, all may be nearly well and good. But it just is not the case, and it never could be the case, that any individual could be completely neutral, completely independent, wholly without preconceptions and moral frameworks for analysis. What this means, it seems to me, is that the responsibility on those who select our judges is a very great one and that, given the importance of retaining the myth of judicial neutrality, that selection needs to be seen to be sound.

CONCLUSION

The relations between judges and politicians will always be fraught. It is hard to exaggerate how deeply the principle of the separation of powers appears to have pervaded the minds of politicians, judges themselves, and commentators who mediate between the people and the political system. The ideal that there should be a clear distinction between those who make the law and those who apply the law is extraordinarily common. Just as sport and politics should not mix, so, it is said, law and politics should also be separate. But they cannot be. Any realistic conception of what is political must embrace some of what courts the world over do. This is not to argue that courts are as powerful as, or – heaven help us – more powerful than legislators or executives, but merely to observe a very obvious fact, a fact that becomes more obvious as the reach of contemporary government extends and the concern for individual rights grow stronger.

To point out that judges, especially in the courts of last resort, may often, and quite properly, act politically is not to say that there is little significant difference between judges and politicians. Their roles in a political system are decidedly different and their methods of operation are distinct. But they are not quite as distinct as some hoary myths might suggest. No serious observer of the major appeal courts in the world subscribes to the view that judges do no more than find the law. Harold Laski tells the story of his attempt to persuade Mr Justice Macnagten that Oliver Wendell Holmes had been correct to argue that, behind every judgement, there lay 'an inarticulate major premise'. Macnagten would have none of it. He recoiled against the whole notion of inarticulacy and was suspicious of complexity. He told Laski that he 'simply applied the law, looking neither to the right nor to the left'.

That is an interesting observation. To start with, it is quite wrong. Nobody can judge hard cases without some theoretical framework to act as a guide. Even a supine obeisance to a conception of parliamentary sovereignty which presumes that all problems related to administrative action can and should be resolved through parliamentary procedures is a theoretical position.

It is interesting, too, in the implication that adjudication can be entirely neutral, cleaving an independent path between the political divisions within society. Of course, sometimes this is true. Much more often, however, any decision will benefit one political persuasion over another and there is no inevitability about which side will benefit. Comparing the Supreme Court under Earl Warren with that under William Rehnquist or contrasting the experiences of Michael Howard with his Labour predecessors in the 1970s makes this point neatly enough.

Nevertheless, there is no escaping the general proposition that courts of last resort do have a bias towards the conservative end of the ideological spectrum. This derives from two sources, the legal principle of *stare decisis*, or keeping to precedents, and the pool from which senior judges are normally selected. Note, however, that this bias is a tendency, not a rule. The United States Supreme Court has always felt able to reverse its precedents and, since the Practice Statement of 1966, so has the British Judicial Committee of the House of Lords. Additionally, where Bills of

Rights exist or access to judicial review is relatively unrestrained, the interests of the less advantaged often prevail. These are not the norm. The usual outcome of a case before the Judicial Committee or the United States Supreme Court (especially where the issue relates to a federal statute) is for the government side to prevail.

The central problem for judges is a problem at the heart of democratic theory. Where the political culture embraces the view that parliamentarians actually represent the People in all their conflicting wishes and the theory that majority wishes have a preferred position on virtually all matters, governments are relatively unconstrained, either by constitutional limitations or by judicial oversight. Republican France before 1958 and the United Kingdom, with its commitment to the sovereignty of Parliament, are the classic instances. By contrast, where the political culture doubts the capacity of representatives to reflect accurately the wishes of the People and fears the power of the state, governments are more formally restrained by constitutional limitations and judiciaries who see their legitimate role as enforcing those limitations.

As times and conditions change, so political theories should change. The expanded role of the state means that the daily lives of the People are increasingly affected by governmental actions. Inevitably, since neither politicians nor bureaucrats are either angels or perfectly consistent, instances arise in large numbers, where there is a need for a redress of grievance. The political branches are too self-interested to perform this function fairly; the judicial branch is the natural place for claims against the state to be heard. If this is accepted, then the courts are inevitably going to be, at times, in conflict with the political branches. If they were not, they would not be doing their job properly.

The relationship between judges and politics will be closely related to the general constitutional theory of a country. Positions can be envisaged as located along a continuum. At one end is a deep concern for individual rights, perhaps at the expense of the majority will and a suspicion of government itself as an instrument of potential coercion, and at the other end is a commitment to the majoritarian principle and a belief in the capacity of government to act on behalf of the People with fairness and efficiency. Judges play an important and active role in the first type of system and a small and passive role in the second. The two extremes are well illustrated by Justice Robert Jackson's powerful defence of the exercise of judicial power in *West Virginia Board of Education v. Barnette* and a Roman question that remains as unanswerable as it is critical.

Jackson wrote: 'The very purpose of a Bill of Rights was to withdraw certain subjects from the vicissitudes of political controversy, to place them beyond the reach of majorities and officials and to establish them as legal principles to be applied by the courts. One's right to life, liberty, and property, to free speech, a free press, freedom or worship and assembly, and other fundamental rights may not be submitted to the vote; they depend on the outcome of no elections'. The Romans, in line with republican France and the mainstream of British thought, worried about the legitimacy of judges finding unlawful the acts of politicians who had gained their positions through the proper channels and could, if they carried out their functions unsatisfactorily, be removed from office. While recognising that judges might be required to become involved in the political world, they doubted their legitimacy. '*Quis custodiet ipsos custodes?*', they asked: Who will guard the guards themselves? And that is, indeed, the conundrum. The separation of powers, properly applied, must grant specific and independent powers to the courts, but reviewing the courts' actions immediately breaks down that separation and reduces the judges' likelihood of acting fairly in a dispute between government and citizen. There are, as I have attempted to show, arguments against relying on citizen democracy, on assembly sovereignty, and on judicial power in any political system. But there is no answer that can square the circle of electoral legitimacy and limited government. All possible ones depend on an inarticulate premise about the nature of democratic government. So all answers will ultimately be political ones.

NOTES ON FURTHER READING

An excellent general introduction to the relationship of the law
to politics, especially in Britain, is Jeremy Waldron, *The Law*
(Routledge, 1990). Two collections of essays with a comparative
perspective are Jerold Waltman and Kenneth M. Holland (eds.),
The Political Role of Law Courts in Modern Democracies (Macmillan,
1988) and Kenneth M. Holland (ed.), *Judicial Activism in
Comparative Perspective* (Macmillan, 1990).

On Britain, there are a handful of useful introductions, nearly all
written by lawyers. Among the best are Marcel Berlins and Clare
Dyer, *The Law Machine* (Penguin, 1994), the classic and
pathbreaking, but now flawed, John Griffiths, *The Politics of the
Judiciary* (Fontana, 1st ed., 1977, 3rd rev'd ed., 1985), the
uniquely insightful (as the Americans would say) Alan Paterson,
The Law Lords (Macmillan, 1992), and the entertaining and
educative pair, David Pannick, *Judges* (Oxford University Press,
1987) and Simon Lee, *Judging Judges* (Faber and Faber, 1988).
Probably the best book by a non-lawyer is Gavin Drewry, *Law,
Justice and Politics* (Longman, 2nd ed., 1981, 1984).

On the United States, the literature is massive. Among the best
introductions remains Robert Jackson's classic *The Supreme Court
in the American System of Government* (Harvard University Press,
1955), but David O'Brien's fine *Storm Center: the Supreme Court
in American Politics* (Norton, 3rd ed., 1994) is more recent and
more detailed. Although much criticized, Bob Woodward and
Scott Armstrong, *The Brethren: inside the Supreme Court* (Simon
and Schuster, 1979), remains a fascinating read; David Savage,

Turning Right? the making of the Rehnquist Supreme Court (John Wiley, 1992) is less full, but good on the early Rehnquist Court, even if a bit journalistic. A sensible and wide-ranging overview is David Barnum, *The Supreme Court and American Democracy* (St. Martin's, 1993) while Robert McKeever, *Raw Judicial Power? the Supreme Court and American Society* (Manchester University Press, 2nd ed., 1995) is more specifically concerned with the Court's recent decisions and their political impact.

INDEX

European Court of Human Rights
(Strasbourg), 1, 10, 49-50
European Court of Justice (ECJ)
(Luxembourg), 1, 10, 74
European Union, 11

Fisher, Lou, 68
France, 1, 20, 27, 42, 86-87
  separation of powers, 12, 49-50, 79-
80, 121, 126
Frankfurter, Felix, 58, 66
Franks, Lord, 120
Frontiero v. Richardson (USA), 107
Fukuyama, Francis, 102

gender discrimination, and US Supreme
Court, 107, 108-109
gender equality, and Brennan, 64
General Electric Company (California),
40-41
Germany, 1, 11-12, 20, 42, 121
Gideon v. Wainwright, 107
Gillick, Victoria, 21
Glazer, Nathan, 3
Goddard, Lord Chief Justice, 72
Goldstone Commission (South Africa),
118-119
Goldwater, Barry, 64
Goodman, Lord, 120
government
  need for checks and balances, 103
  question of modern role, 115
Greater London Council (GLC), 17, 35,
89
Griffiths, John, 88, 89, 122

Hamilton, Alexander, 47, 99
health care, question of expense and
efficacy, 68
Heaton Transport Ltd v. TGWU (UK),
50, 62
Hoffman, Lord, 91-92
Holmes, Oliver Wendell, 30, 124-125
House of Commons, select committees,
97

House of Lords
  Judicial Committee, 6, 20, 28, 51, 126
    conventions and procedure, 53-54,
56, 61-62
      education, 91-92
      and precedent, 93-94, 125
Howard, Michael, 1, 5, 42, 70, 73-74,
75, 99
Hoyt, Jennifer, 108-109
Hurd, Douglas, 6

immigration, 113
individual, recognition of rights of, 18
interest groups, involvement in litigation,
40-43
Irangate scandal, US enquiries into, 119-
120
Ireland, 26-27
Ireland, Northern, 118
Irish Republican Army, 5
Irvine, Lord, 9

Jackson, Robert, 33, 38, 127
Jauncey, Lord, 91
Jefferson, Thomas, 56
Jeffreys, Judge, 71
Johnson, Lyndon, 48
Johnson v. Santa Clara County (USA),
108
judges
  enquiries into disasters and political
embarrassments, 117-119
  as officials, accountability, 97-98
  question of history of previous political
involvement, 27
  question of role, bias and legitimacy of
status, 72-73
  relationship with politics, 127
  see also United Kingdom; United States
Judges' Council, and sentencing, 7-8
judicial review, 9, 111, 113-114
judiciary
  question of essential role, 102
  question of relationship with
legislature, 105-106

ALSO PUBLISHED IN THE BOWERDEAN BRIEFINGS SERIES

CONTROLLING THE ARMS TRADE
THE WEST *VERSUS* THE REST
by PAUL CORNISH

This book examines the development of the international arms trade after the Cold War and looks at efforts – national and international – to regulate or restrain the market. The book describes the size and dynamics of the international market for weapons and related technology. Who are the main suppliers and purchasers of conventional arms? What is meant by 'dual-use' technology? What effect – if any – has the so-called 'peace dividend' had upon the manufacture and export of lethal weaponry? Much has been said, since the end of the Cold War, of the need to regulate the market. In Britain, what are likely to be the implications of the Scott Report into arms and technology exports to Iraq? *Controlling the Arms Trade* is an informed and authoritative pointer to future market trends and a clear and concise guide to the problem of arms export controls.

Dr Paul Cornish is Senior Research Fellow at the Royal Institute of International Affairs. He served in the British Army's Royal Tank Regiment from 1983-89, and spent two years as arms trade analyst at the Foreign Office in London, 1991-93. *The Arms Trade and Europe* was published by Pinter/RIIA in December 1995, and *British Military Planning for the Defence of Germany, 1945-50* was published by Macmillan in January 1996.

ISBN: 0 906097 44 4   EXTENT: 128 pp   PRICE: £9.99

RETREAT FROM THE MODERN
– HUMANISM, POST-MODERNISM AND THE FLIGHT FROM MODERNIST CULTURE
by N.J. RENGGER

A short but entertaining *tour d'horizon* of the factions and theories competing for high ground in the so-called culture wars. Dr Rengger takes us confidently through the conflicting (but also sometimes overlapping) positions that constitute the Modernist debate – from the Enlightenment through to post-modernism, via high humanism, pluralism, multiculturalism and anti-humanism.

In a wide-ranging discussion Dr Rengger deals with the work of all the foremost contributors to the debate, from Pico della Mirandola and the Baron Condorcet to Adorno, Steiner, Rorty, Habermas, Heidegger, Foucault, Derrida, Said, Bloom, Fish and others. Anyone who needs to know more about the meaning of terms such as structuralism, post-modernism or deconstruction will find this book an invaluable guide.

N.J. Rengger is Reader in Political Theory and International Relations at the University of St Andrews. He has published widely in contemporary political theory, intellectual history, cultural theory and international ethics. His most recent book is *Political Theory, Modernity and Post-Modernity: Beyond Enlightenment and Critique* (B Blackwell, 1995). He is currrently working on the interrelationship of culture and responsibility in international ethics.

ISBN: 0 906097 29 0 EXTENT:128pp PRICE: £9.99

THE POLITICS OF AIDS
by VIRGINIA VAN DER VLIET.

Great plagues have always brought out the best and the worst in human nature. Which is more prevalent in any society at any time will depend in part on the attitudes and policies it adopts.

In *The Politics of AIDS* Virginia van der Vliet shows how markedly attitudes towards this twentieth-century plague vary from country to country in accordance with differing religious convictions and as a result of social customs and prejudice.

In particular, she draws attention to the predicament of women in the poorest Third World countries, pointing out that by 1992, of the 11. 8 million adults believed to be HIV-infected, 40% – or 4.7 million – were women.

How this has arisen, the likely consequences, and the outlook in general for the spread or containment of the AIDS epidemic throughout the world are the subjects of this stimulating and important book.

Virginia van der Vliet is a social anthropologist. She trained at the University of Witwatersrand and taught at Rhodes University from 1963 to 1980 and at the University of Cape Town between 1981 and 1990. She has written on demography, urban African marriage, and, more recently, on the AIDS epidemic in South Africa.

ISBN: 0 906097 24 X EXTENT: 160pp. PRICE: £9.99